Praise for The Confident Introvert

Enhancing the Quality of Life

This delightful travel adventure by superb guide, Lynette Crane, can help millions of people who live their lives socially isolated from the Human Connection. She takes all those who identify themselves as "shy" or "introverted" on a new, easy to follow journey toward personal fulfillment and happiness. Her advice, that is sensitively and interestingly given, can lead to significant enhancements in the quality of life of all those who wish to thrive not merely to survive.

~ Philip Zimbardo, Ph.D., Professor Emeritus Stanford University, Author of *Shyness: What It Is, What To Do About It*

A Must Read!

The Confident Introvert has the power to change the way introverts see themselves and equips them with practical skills to turn their personality into a winning asset. Introvert or not, there is something to glean for everyone as we all would be wise to recognize our own inner, unique strengths and learn how to exert them effectively. If you have ever felt misunderstood for being an introvert, READ THIS BOOK!

~ Nancy O'Reilly, Psy.D., Speaker, Therapist, Founder and Director of WomenSpeak Project (www.womenspeak.com) and WomenConnect4Good Foundation

Invaluable Handbook

I hadn't realized before that there can be such a person as a shy extrovert, and also that not all introverts are shy. Before reading this book, I thought shyness and introversion were much the same thing, but not so! Author Lynette Crane explores and explains the relationship between self-esteem and shyness in a way that can be understood by anyone. Defining shyness is one of the first steps towards dealing with it. This book does that expertly, and goes on to offer applicable solutions. A very helpful handbook that I will read more than once.

~ Nadia Giordana, Author, Speaker, Host of WomanVision TV, website: www.EmbodyYourVision.com

Fabulous!

I love this book! It is very thorough and also very readable. It is a valuable tool and also a validation for all of us who want to express ourselves more clearly and to understand where communications may have gone wrong.

~ Marilyn King, Ph.D., Mediation/Arbitration/Settlement Coordinator, Retired Psychologist

A World of Possibilities

The Confident Introvert is a book that made me think about things I hadn't thought about before. For instance, what does it mean to be a "confident introvert"? Doesn't that sound like an oxymoron? Except, I'm finding out through Coach Lynette Crane that one can be an introvert and be confident at the same time! Who knew? I was unprepared for the wealth of information and insight that *The Confident Introvert* opened up to me. I love the personal anecdotes, which drew me to the book in the first place. Coach Lynette Crane is living proof that a person with heart and passion can begin to live the life that we all wish we could live: to be healthy in mind and in spirit and enjoy life to the fullest by not letting society define and determine who we are. As Marcel Proust once wrote, "The real voyage of discovery consists not in seeking new lands, but in seeing with new eyes." There are no boxes in Lynette's world, only a world of possibilities. Pick up a copy of *The Confident Introvert* and begin to open your eyes and see anew.

~ Mia Jones, ComputerCats

Best-Kept Secret

I read half of your book already. I was reading on a bus, I just couldn't stop! And I know already that I will read it again and again.

You are the best-kept secret, Lynette!!! My jaw was hanging all my trip, hehe! You took all the science and psychology and put [them] together, so anyone without psychological background can understand and USE!!

I always thought that it is clear that my, "Would you like to go and get some coffee?" means I want coffee!! Now I see that some people just don't get indirect communication. Cannot wait to read it all! Thank you!!!

~ Jurate "Jade" Janusauske, Social Media Manager

Understanding Introverts *and* Extroverts

"I read Lynette Crane's excellent book, *The Confident Introvert*, while preparing for an interview with her on my Hope, Healing and WellBeing internet radio show. I found her book to be invaluable for anyone who wants to be more reflective and proactive regarding their introverted personality. Lynette not only describes characteristics like shyness, but she provides helpful advice for introverts to deal with various situations including taking risks and handling both praise and criticism effectively. As an extrovert, I also appreciated the excellent advice for how to be more supportive of the introverts I work with, live with and love. I highly recommend *The Confident Introvert* for anyone seeking to better understand the introverted side within themselves and others."

~ Mary Treacy O'Keefe, M.A., President, Well Within

The Confident Introvert
Gain the Skills to Overcome Shyness and Low Self-Esteem

For unconfident introverts, shy extroverts, and anyone who wishes to gain the freedom and joy of a full life while remaining true to yourself

Lynette Crane

∞

Cover design by Alan Michael Design, Minneapolis,
Minnesota

Published by Creative Life Changes, Minneapolis,
Minnesota

Edited by Blue Lotus Editing, San Francisco,
California

This book is dedicated to James Andrews, whose wit and wisdom continue to illuminate my life.

Acknowledgements

My deepest thanks to:

Dr. Philip Zimbardo, whose groundbreaking research on shyness first set me on this path, and whose books on shyness were my first teaching texts;

Connie Anderson, the editor who did the first important critical run-through of the book and provided the insights of a non-introvert;

My editor and inspiring spiritual friend, Marilyn King, for her unflagging work, dedication to important minutiae, and for her ability to correct me and somehow make me like it;

My sister, Diane Roy, who claims never to have seen me shy, but who has always supported my endeavors, including this one;

My coach, Pat Mussieux, whose insistence that people really needed to hear what I had to say finally convinced even this introvert;

Susan Cain, whose book, *Quiet: The Power of Introverts in a World That Can't Stop Talking,* helped raise my self-esteem to towering heights;

And to the many friends who have tolerated my hibernation and cheered me on as I labored to produce this book.

Table of Contents

Foreword

Some years ago I joined a discussion group which consisted of people who had been together for several years, were deeply into the topic and had bonded with each other.

I joined the group after a serious illness, and for the first few meetings, I was relatively quiet, preferring to listen to what others had to say, as I had not yet developed my thoughts on the topic. Eventually, I took off, and became a deeply involved, frequent contributor.

After about a year, several people commented on how "shy" I had been when I came into the group, but I was "much better now." This was always said with an air of approval, but I was furious.

Part of my fury was due to the fact that I in fact had been shy for much of my life, but believed I had overcome it successfully. Suddenly, I was "outed" in public. But I wondered, why is it socially acceptable to make a public comment like that to another human being, one that those of us who have suffered from shyness experience as hurtful and demeaning? Does the speaker believe it is being helpful to point this out? Is it a backhanded compliment? Would it be acceptable to say to someone, "You were so aggressive when I first met you, but you're better now?" or, "I thought you were so boastful when you came into the group, but you've changed?" I don't believe so. Being quiet and being a good listener may be qualities valued in some cultures, but the United States does not seem to be one of them.

My journey from shyness to confidence has not changed the fact that I am, at heart, an introvert, nor will it change the fact that I still believe that listening to others first when in a new environment is an intelligent way to proceed.

So I have listened to many shy people or those who are judged, rightly or wrongly, to be shy. Besides being tired of being asked, "Why are you so quiet?" the complaint I hear most often from introverts or shy people is this: "I don't want to feel I have something wrong with me and that I need to be 'fixed.'"

Even worse is this plaintive question I sometimes get: "Do you think there's a cure for shyness?" A *cure?* As in disease?

Those of us who have made the journey from insecurity to security know the change is possible; we also know that in order to do so, it is necessary to make a few changes in our own behavior – not in our preferences for quiet pleasures and one-on-one relationships, but in the ways in which we connect with others and let them know, subtly, who we really are and how we want to be treated.

I don't think there is anything inherently "wrong" with shy people, and I especially don't think of shyness as a disease, but I do think there is something wrong with a world in which the comments, talents, and contributions of shy people, who now constitute a growing portion of our society, are often overlooked. Unfortunately, sensitizing the whole world to quieter, more introverted people is not possible; therefore, it is the challenge of the shy person to learn how to make others aware of his or her fine qualities, at the same time maintaining an allegiance to that inner core that values quiet and privacy.

This book is for those people who are highly motivated to have a freer, more joyful life, are willing to make the effort to get it, but don't want to try to turn into someone they don't recognize.

It is also for those who have never felt shy but who, for some reason, have read this far. If you are motivated to do so, you can open up a whole new world of understanding of a group of people who are often loaded with imagination, creativity, and talent, but who will never shout it in your face. But you can hear what they have to say if you are willing to be still and to listen.

Introduction

Success, awards and recognition, compliments, a perfect body, enviable possessions, and positive relationships – every one of us has spent a part of our lives reaching for one or more of these things. Some of us spend more time than others grasping for that *one* thing or event that will finally convince us "we are all right."

At times, we convince ourselves we have at last reached a place of safety – a relationship, a job, a dream home – only to find how vulnerable we are when the situation changes.

Years ago, I was extremely fearful to end a toxic relationship, and realized that I believed I had no skills to help me find a new one. And, I was convinced that I'd never even have the opportunity to do so.

It was then I was forced to review my life that had been crippled for some years by shyness. Here is one example of my early experiences:

As a youngster, I attended dance class several days a week after school. Carrying my schoolbooks and my dance bag, I climbed onto one of San Francisco's cable cars for the trip to my dance studio. Several blocks before my stop, I began to look around wildly and to perspire heavily. Why? The uninitiated guess that I was uneasy about performing in my dance class, but surprisingly enough, many shy people are at ease performing a well-loved skill, even in public.

Those who are very familiar either with shyness – or with San Francisco's cable cars – may guess the real reason. On a cable car, you have no cord to pull, no button to push, to inform the operator that you wish to get off. I had to raise my voice and call out from my seat, "Franklin Street, please!" For a shy person like me, this was so threatening that it was easier to wait until someone else got off and then follow. I frequently rode several blocks beyond my stop and had to walk back, carrying my heavily loaded dance bag.

A shy person's daily life is filled with such torments, minor and major. It's true: shy people work too hard. We don't ask for help, don't ask for directions, and don't ask for the things we want and need.

And we don't let others know how we want to be treated, nor how we *don't* want to be treated. Most of all we don't think very much of our own worth or feel very optimistic about the future, because to us daily life consists of a myriad of failures which seem to stretch on and on into infinity. The conversations we have in our heads about ourselves would drive away our best friends if they were the targets of such comments.

So what happens as the result of shyness and low self-esteem? Poorer intimate relationships, a lack of adequate support groups, an inability to make our talents really flower, and consequently, more depression and poorer health.

Shyness doesn't fade away naturally with age, like "baby fat." Applause, awards, degrees, and other achievements had not driven out my low self-esteem. No matter how much I longed to shut out the daily dread and unlock the feeling of ease, no one person seemed to have the key to help.

On a gloomy day in 1983, facing my fear to leave that toxic relationship, I reviewed my life as a prisoner of shyness, telling myself that this was just a problem, like any other. I had successfully performed on stage as a dancer, completed college summa cum laude, been elected to Phi Beta Kappa, obtained a graduate degree, and had been a popular teacher for 13 years. Surely, if I could solve all of those problems, I could solve this one.

My search for what we shy people really need resulted in a class I created called "Shyness and Self Esteem." This book is written from my real-life experiences and the invaluable insights I obtained from working semester after semester with others who had similarly suffered.

The class was filled with what we *do* really need, based on the notion that happiness and a release from the prison of shyness and low self-esteem comes through attaining the *skills* needed to bring about a happy life. It's not about getting "A's" for effort. It is about making the right effort to learn the right skills.

This book is based on what I learned from that class, and about the skills we need to:

- Connect with others in a way that enhances our lives
- Develop our talents
- Be recognized for our excellence
- Have the resiliency to handle the fact that we will sometimes get an "F" in life
- Understand that the world does not end when we do occasionally fail

Once we are able to do all this easily, we will find our reservoir of self-esteem filled to the brim, and our shyness fading as a faint, but no longer painful memory.

If you've ever continued to eat your favorite comfort food even when you were uncomfortably full, spent too much money on things that clutter your home more than they bring you pleasure, or pursued a relationship with someone who really didn't make you feel very good, you have experienced what it is like to fill the "hole" in your life with things that don't make the difference you want.

As a wise friend of mine once remarked, "You can never get enough of what you don't really need."

What human beings need are supportive relationships and the knowledge that what they do makes a difference in the world.

Let us get started now on acquiring some of the things we really do need.

Chapter One:
What are Shyness and Self-Esteem?

In an article I read some years ago, I'll never forget how the author described his idea of self-esteem, and why he was so resistant to the term. It seems that when he heard the term "self-esteem," he pictured the kind of guy who strides through the airport talking loudly and importantly on his cell phone, while he bumps into other people or accidentally trips them. If this was his picture of high self-esteem, who knows how he would have defined low self-esteem, but I suspect that it was of a quieter, politer person.

There seems to be continuing confusion about the term "self-esteem" – the evaluations of self-worth that can be low, high, or somewhere in between, and may fluctuate with different situations.

Self-Esteem as Competence

Over one hundred years ago, the American psychologist and philosopher William James wrote that self-esteem is actually the result of perceived success, or competence, in an area that is important to the person.

A more recent and widely accepted definition has been proposed by psychotherapist Nathaniel Branden, who defines self-esteem as not only being confident that you are competent to cope with the basic challenges of life, but of feeling worthy of being happy, believing that achievement, success, love, respect, and fulfillment are appropriate to you.

Self-Esteem as Problem Solving

Noted psychologist Albert Bandura has identified something he calls "self-efficacy": "the *belief* in one's capabilities to organize and execute the courses of action required to manage prospective situations." This seems to be a fine description of healthy self-esteem.

According to Bandura (1994), people with a strong sense of self-efficacy:
- View challenging problems as tasks to be mastered
- Develop deeper interest in the activities in which they participate
- Form a stronger sense of commitment to their interests and activities
- Recover quickly from setbacks and disappointments

People with a weak sense of self-efficacy:
- Avoid challenging tasks
- Believe that difficult tasks and situations are beyond their capabilities
- Focus on personal failings and negative outcomes
- Quickly lose confidence in personal abilities

To put it another way, self-esteem might be seen as the process by which you evaluate yourself and your actions, predict the future, and make judgments about yourself and others. And then you make it come true.

If we think of high self-esteem as consisting of 1) positive evaluations of yourself, 2) based on experiences you have set up, 3) that guide you in selecting goals and the paths to those goals, and 4) allow you to predict a positive future, then we can begin to develop a map you can use to reach that desired state.

The good news is that "the growth of self-efficacy continues to evolve throughout life as people acquire new skills, experiences, and understanding (Bandura, 1992)."

There are clues to self-esteem – high and low – in the outward behavior of others. Below are some examples:

- *Michael was a young man who was stunningly handsome, impeccably dressed, and most of all, dazzlingly bright. Born into a wealthy family, he had every opportunity in the world available to him. His suicide was a complete, and awful, surprise. Suicide of this privileged young person was the last thing onlookers would have predicted.*

- *Beatrice was a petite, slender, bright woman with piquant charm and a flashing wit. Gifted artistically, she filled her life and her home with her lovely creations.*

  Very few people outside her family knew of her talents, however, because she did not show her works to others. As a student in an art class, she went to shows displaying the works of her fellow students, but declined to offer hers. Why? Her fear of criticism and rejection was so great that it was too great a risk. Unfortunately, she never heard the praise she coveted, either, because she made sure that very few people saw her work. At the end of her life, she remarked bitterly that she had never gotten support for her talent.

Both of these people had extremely low self-esteem, a sense of such poor self-worth that they were blind to the love, acceptance, and other gifts the world was ready to bestow upon them. What were they waiting for? What did they need to hear, or have happen, in order to feel worthy?

If X Happens, *then* I'll Feel Good about Myself

Many people are convinced that a specific event will bring about the magical change: *If* I get a college degree, *then* I'll feel good about myself ... *When* I lose weight, find a lover, establish a home, *then* I'll feel secure ... *When* others recognize my abilities, *then* I'll know I'm a success ....

If, by some miracle, the goal is reached, another one is usually set up to take its place, thus forever postponing the miraculous change.

- *Beatrice had reached many goals often coveted by other people. She was physically very lovely, quite intelligent, and had married a man who was the "catch of the day" who supported her talents. Somehow it wasn't enough. She needed to have her artwork praised lavishly and be desired by significant other people, with no threat whatsoever of criticism, before she would dare to display it. This never happened, of course, because if you exhibit your dreams or your creations, you will always face challenges – as well as acceptance.*

- *Michael's needs were less clear, but like Beatrice, he exhibited a major symptom that would alert anyone who was really knowledgeable about self-esteem: both of them were highly critical of other people. They were so critical, in fact, that they made everyone around them uncomfortable and afraid they would violate some standard of speech, dress, or behavior that would bring a sharp comment.*

Characteristics of High Self-Esteem

People with high self-esteem seem to make others around them feel safe. That is not to say that they do not have standards, nor that they do not correct other people, when appropriate. But they know *how* to do so, and *when* to do so, in ways that are helpful to others. These will be some of the skills we will explore in this book.

What is the Relationship of Shyness to Self-Esteem?

Shyness is never found in combination with high self-esteem. Low self-esteem may manifest itself in many ways – shy withdrawal, aggressive bluster, or clown-like comedy – but never as relaxed, confident behavior.

What is Shyness?

The foremost researcher in this field, Philip Zimbardo, defines shyness as a *feeling of discomfort that keeps you from saying or doing what you really want to say or do.* This feeling must be based on thoughts about oneself, and results in behaviors that we label as "shy."

Dr. Zimbardo's research demonstrated that, starting in the 1970's, 40 percent of the U.S. population was chronically shy, another 40 percent of people reported having been previously shy, while 15 percent experienced shyness in some situations. Only 5 percent described themselves as never shy. We are talking about a disorder that is life-altering as it affects one's success in all areas of life. Shyness afflicts a high proportion of the population. Furthermore, it may be thought of as "contagious"; parents who lack basic social and problem-solving skills fail to teach them to their children. And people with low self-esteem, especially those in authority, such as teachers and bosses, unwittingly create the same patterns of low self-esteem in those they oversee. Some of the ways they do this to others, particularly children, is by being overly critical or incapable of recognizing individual differences, important differences that may contribute to the strength of a family, a team, or a society.

The key in determining whether behavior is or is not a characteristic of shyness is: Do you feel you have a *choice*?

Introversion and shyness aren't the same thing

"Introvert" and "shy" aren't the same thing. Shyness should not be confused with being an introvert (introversion). The introvert tends to be more reserved, have smaller circles of friends, and prefer solitary activities, but doesn't necessarily fear social encounters. The extrovert prefers social activities to solitary activities, and is outgoing, gregarious, assertive, and seeks stimulation.

In 1989, psychologist Jerome Kagan and colleagues commenced a long-term study, starting with a group of over 5000 infants, exposing them to many different kinds of stimuli and stimulus change, including popping balloons. Twenty percent of the babies, whom he called "high-reactive," responded strongly to the stimuli, crying and pumping their arms vigorously. Another forty percent stayed relatively quiet, and forty percent were somewhere in between those two extremes.

Upon following up over the years, as he predicted, he found that the babies who were high-reactive matured into introverted adolescents.

Introversion is not the result of social anxiety. It is merely a social preference – a choice. Why? Because the introvert's own inner life and imagination are stimulating enough. Elaine Aron, in her 1997 book, *The Highly Sensitive Person*, maintains that introverts have a lower threshold for stimulation, which drains their energy, and therefore they learn to protect themselves by keeping a low profile. Some of the qualities she believes are clues to introversion include being aware of subtle changes in the environment, being very sensitive to environmental stimulation including coffee consumption, feeling overwhelmed when asked to do too many different things at the same time, and needing to withdraw to refill the "energy tanks."

Introverts may prefer one-on-one conversations to group activities, and feel more comfortable expressing themselves in writing.

On the plus side, they are often good listeners, dedicated and conscientious workers, and can concentrate easily. And they can become superb performers.

A study by K. Anders Ericsson indicated that introversion may lie behind outstanding performance in many fields, from music and athletics to chess. In one study, he and his colleagues at the Music Academy in Berlin asked professors to divide violinists into groups, predicting those who would go on to a professional career and those who were more likely to become teachers instead of performers.

All the violinists spent approximately the same amount of time practicing, but those whose skill levels predicted they would play well enough to perform publicly spent the bulk of their time practicing – alone.

Extroverts, who seem to prefer a great deal of stimulation, including social stimulation, are presumably less comfortable making that commitment to hours of solitary practice.

- *Elsa was a superb pianist; everyone around her predicted a brilliant performing career. However, Elsa, a very passionate and outgoing young woman and an extrovert, had great trouble spending the hours alone that she needed to devote to her practice. She would have great bouts of depression and crying, which were "cured" when she was able to go outside and socialize.*

  The great career never happened; instead, she became a fine musician who delighted in playing for her friends in her living room. But she was unable to face the long hours of practice, and the many solitary journeys to concert halls that would have been part of her professional career.

Although introversion is not the same as shyness, introverts are frequently "told" in one way or another by those around them that there is something wrong with them. "You're so quiet" is a frequent comment that indicates criticism of the introvert. Faced with constant feedback that there is something wrong with them, it is easy for an introvert to also be shy.

Here's what one introvert has to say about her choices that honor her need for low stimulation in her life: *"It's like keeping the door to your apartment closed when you're inside and being made to feel strange for it."*

And consider this poignant example from an introvert who would like to be understood: *"Recently people have been questioning me as to why I like going out and exploring things alone. They get upset that they don't get invited and I find it very frustrating that outside of work, I am not able to enjoy myself without the need to worry about what other people think. Am I selfish 90% of the time? I enjoy the freedom of my own company."*

The Shy Extrovert

These people are privately shy, unlike the publicly shy whose shy characteristics can be visible to others. Shy extroverts can carry on the necessary social activities in structured situations or in situations where they are in control, for example, as a performer, a public speaker, or a teacher. In each of these cases, the person has a "script" to follow and can look very confident, even relaxed, provided that there is no deviation from the script.

Their shyness is based on the underlying fear that what they feel is their personally inadequate "real self" might be exposed accidentally in more unstructured, spontaneous, or intimate situations. In short, they may have perfected their skills in the area of performance, but be totally unprepared for the easy give-and-take of daily conversation.

Some shy extroverts may even intimidate others, perhaps in an effort to keep other people at arm's length.

- *Phil seemed very energetic and outgoing on the surface, but he had real doubts about his value, including his intelligence, which was, in fact, very high. During conversations with others, Phil would frequently (and suddenly) introduce a new topic on which he was an expert, but others were not. It kept everyone else a little off balance, and helped Phil temporarily achieve the sensation of superiority rather than inferiority. He may even have convinced the less secure of his listeners of his intellectual superiority.*

Many a fan has been puzzled to discover that a performer who has dazzled, charmed, and amused them seems curiously aloof up close, when the artificial barrier between performer and audience is eliminated.

The media are filled with stories of the marital and addiction problems of brilliantly talented people who have apparently not solved the basic problem of how to live in harmony with themselves and with others.

Confidence isn't all it's cracked up to be

Shy people, and even non-shy introverts, may envy the confident extrovert, but no one type need be envied without reservations. True extroverts may be overly confident, with an inflated sense of their own abilities.

According to research conducted by Dr. Briony Pulford and Professor Andrew Coleman of the University of Leicester, in collaboration with Dr. Fergus Bolger of the University of Durham, overconfidence among businesspeople is a reason why many ventures fail in the first few years. And the ones most culpable were people with absolute confidence in their abilities.

The researchers set up a "game" that simulated market conditions. Participants stood to gain capital, or take a loss, depending decisions they made in different market scenarios. The players had to choose, given different market scenarios, whether or not to open restaurants. Both skill and luck played a role in performance. However, said Dr. Pulford, "Our results showed that, when success depended on <u>skill</u>, overconfidence tended to cause excess entry into a market place. Market entry decisions tend to be over-optimistic ... and many new businesses fail within a few years."

In other words, everyone who looks supremely confident isn't necessarily destined for success.

<u>Anti-social behavior is not shy behavior</u>

Some people wrongly think of shy people as anti-social. The term "anti-social" is defined in the *American Psychiatric Association's Diagnostic and Statistical Manual* as "a pervasive pattern of disregard for, and violation of, the rights of others that begins in childhood or early adolescence and continues into adulthood." Symptoms can include persistent lying and/or stealing, impulsivity, recklessness, inability to stay in school or to hold a job, and a noticeable lack of remorse for harming others. Hardly a description of a shy person!

Some Outward Signals of Shyness

<u>Low speaking voice or not talking</u>

Shy people are frequently locked in a prison of shyness, afraid to offer opinions, protest, or ask for information or assistance for fear of appearing foolish and experiencing rejection.

However, being quiet is in itself not necessarily a sign of shyness. Jake had high self-esteem, but he was able to relax and listen quietly to others who had expertise or opinions very different from his. In this manner, he had gathered an astonishing amount of information about the world. Originally trained as a military intelligence officer, Jake had incorporated this training into his civilian life to broaden his horizons and develop an astonishing network of friends.

A very confident person may be extremely relaxed and a good listener. By contrast, in a similar situation a shy person may be preoccupied with an internal dialogue that includes, "I *should* have something to say. They're going to think I'm a dummy. If I say something, maybe I will be seen as ridiculous," and so on. But the anxious person is not really listening to others.

Once again, the question is: Do you feel have a choice?

If self-esteem and shyness are *thought* processes, what is their impact on behavior? By what means do they affect behavior?

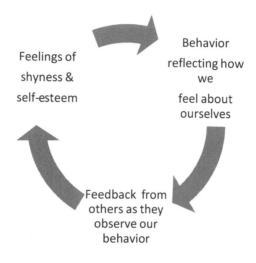

The Vicious Circle

Social withdrawal

Shyness is a phenomenon that is triggered by social interaction, or the thought of social interaction. Fears of rejection, shame, or ridicule cause shy people to reject experiences involving others, thus imprisoning themselves in isolation.

Note what happens in the "Vicious Circle" (above): Low self-esteem results in behavior that is interpreted by others as withdrawal or even rejection of social interaction. The result is that others interpret this behavior as a desire to be left alone, or even a rejection of them, and leave the shy person firmly alone. The shy person interprets the feedback as rejection! It was this circle that prompted Zimbardo to compare shyness to a prison in which the shy person is both the prisoner – and the jailer.

The social mistakes that shy people fear making do not in themselves isolate the shy person from others. It is the shy person's reaction to the mistake that makes the difference.

- *Harold attended the first meeting of the German Club at his college. As the president of the club approached to greet him, Harold took a step backwards and knocked the punch bowl, which spilled all over the table. After helping to clean up, Harold fled the club and never returned. Upon meeting the president on campus a week later, Harold mumbled "hello" and dropped his eyes as he scurried past. His thought: "They must really think I'm a clumsy jerk."*

- *Janie, on the other hand, attended her first club meeting and dropped a plate of cake down the front of her neighbor's dress. She blushed, apologized nicely, and told herself, "Anyone can make a mistake. I was very nervous because I was meeting these people for the first time." Then she put the incident behind her and tried to focus on what others were saying. Later in the year, she was elected an officer of the club.*

Janie had learned a very important lesson. If she had obsessed about her mistake, she would have behaved awkwardly when she met the same people again. Her awkward behavior *would* have done two things: 1) preoccupied her so much with pictures of possible mistakes that she would be far more likely to do something else clumsy; and 2) subtly made others around her uncomfortable with her discomfort, thereby avoiding her. Isn't this awkward?

Perfectionism

People with low self-esteem are often afflicted with perfectionism, believing that if they can just be perfect in appearance and behavior all the time, they will escape criticism, and as a consequence, rejection. The burden of perfectionism is a lot like always carrying around a tray of fragile glassware, needing to maintain balance at all times, and having to be aware at every moment of the possibility of damage to this burden of being perfect. Danger is everywhere. It doesn't leave that person with much energy to be spontaneous, relaxed, or to connect warmly with others.

Poor eye contact

There are strong cultural differences in what constitutes appropriate eye contact. In American corporate culture, inability to make what is considered to be appropriate eye contact is interpreted as dishonesty and/or inadequacy – and, of course, shyness. (See Chapter 6 on making confident eye contact.)

Fidgeting

Hair twisting and twirling, nail biting, unconscious little body slumps, and dissatisfied facial expressions that communicate a sense of failure are all ways that betray the self-conscious.

Rigid posture

The opposite of slumping, too strict adherence to a concept of "good posture" can also signal a sense of uneasiness. Relaxed people *look* relaxed.

Garbled speech

One of the greatest fears of people, even those who don't label themselves as "shy," is the fear of sounding ridiculous. In fact, it is said that the number one fear in the United States is of public speaking, where the chance of sounding ridiculous is magnified by the size of the audience.

Garbled speech may take the form of stuttering, reversing word order, or echoing the original speaker.

- *Bart was in awe of the owner of the company where he worked. One day, while walking in the hall, he saw Mr. Moss coming towards him in an otherwise empty hall. When Mr. Moss said, "Hi, Bart, how's it going?" Bart replied brightly, "Very thank you fine."*

- *Lucinda called Anne about a new order. When Anne answered the telephone, Lucinda said, "Hi, Anne, how are you?" Anne quickly echoed brightly, "Hi, Anne, how are you?" and then choked, blushing.*

Excessive perspiration

A sure sign of stress, excessive perspiration becomes particularly troublesome when it even affects the palms of the hands, making meeting and greeting people with a handshake most embarrassing!

Blushing – the most apparent signal

Why do we do it? One theory is that it is a response that developed because we are social animals. We blush because we realize we have made a social mistake, and are sorry for it. In this theory, blushing is a part of emotional intelligence.

Blushing develops when we enter school, and become involved in larger social situations than our immediate family. Blushing is so apparent to onlookers that people who blush easily even develop a fear of blushing.

There is no easy remedy for blushing. Developing the skills with which to handle new situations will reduce the fear that triggers blushing: the idea that we have made a painful mistake and must somehow apologize for it.

Situational vs. Chronic Shyness

Chronic shyness occurs in all, or most settings. Shyness that occurs only in certain settings or with certain people is called "situational shyness."

- *Jim was a very confident leader who was able to express himself firmly and with great passion in public settings, such as work or union meetings. He was a strong advocate of excellent public education, and fairness for working people.*

  He was embarrassed to admit that being in the presence of wealthy people in fancy dress made him shy and reluctant to speak up. He didn't know why this happened to him.

Some Clues to Low Self-Esteem

Emphasis on criticism

Shy people are intensely critical of themselves, monitoring their every move for some flaw that might cause them to experience rejection. With this critical view of the world, it is no wonder that they believe others look constantly for flaws. Sometimes the person with low self-esteem becomes very critical of others.

In the absence of any other outward signs of shyness or low self-esteem, remember that someone who looks very self-confident, but who might leave others feeling a little inadequate, is probably not a good example of high self-esteem. The essence of high self-esteem is not only to feel good about yourself, but also to help others, or at least allow them, when in your presence, to also feel good about themselves.

Excessively affected by praise and criticism

Life becomes an emotional roller-coaster ride, as the self-conscious often respond too strongly to the reactions of others. The person's self-perception is similar to that of someone who is wandering through a funhouse filled with distorting mirrors, at times seeing a grossly elongated body, at other times a short person with an extremely long neck, etc.

People with low self-esteem are too much at the mercy of other people and their opinions. A part of maturity lies in learning to evaluate yourself and your work in ways that are useful to your progress, and to seek helpful feedback from the right people in meeting your goals. (See Chapter 5 on criticism and self-evaluation.)

Action steps for Chapter 1:

1. Shy people have often grown up in an excessively critical environment, and as a consequence of having this negative model, tend to become critical of themselves and of others. What's worse, they may have come to believe that the entire world is a critical place in which they will only experience negative judgments. If this has been your experience, try the following

exercise designed to take the focus off yourself and self-consciousness and open your eyes to the positive aspects of the world.

Note that this initial exercise doesn't require you to do anything that is apparent to others – just pay attention to the world around you.

For one week, mentally note a *positive descriptive feature* of each person you meet. No negatives ("fat" or "old") or generalizations, such as racial or ethnic identity. Make a note of what you were able to recognize as positive, such as generous, or good-humored, and about how you felt when doing this exercise.

We will build on this exercise in later chapters.

Chapter Two:
Why Me?

The paradox of shyness is that the shy person feels isolated in his or her discomfort, when in fact, shy people have a lot of company. The first research in the 1970's on shyness by Dr. Zimbardo found that four in ten people in the United States were chronically shy; they reported that it affected their lives negatively on a frequent basis. A sad five percent of those defined themselves as shy all of the time, in all situations, and with all people.

Prevalence of Shyness

Culture affects rates of shyness. The United States did not have the lowest or the highest rates of shyness. Research in other countries revealed something interesting: cultures, such as Japan's, that punished failure with shame as a part of their socialization techniques, had higher rates of shyness. In a culture such as Israel's, where it is not as shameful to try and fail, shyness rates were much lower.

Cultural factors in recent years have changed the figures in the United States.

Shyness has been on the rise, with almost half of the U.S. population now describing themselves as chronically shy. And a major reason may be our increasingly technological society with automated cash machines, stamp vending machines and gas pumps that take credit cards, and even automated check-out lines at the grocery store. The result? No interaction with another human being; no way to ask questions, no casual exchange of social pleasantries, and no way to practice standing up for yourself.

Young people frequently interact more with computers. When they do interact with friends and family, it is likely to be reading e-mail or texting. Instead of there being give-and-take exchanges of information, conversations are more likely to be written, like telegrams.

More and more people are working at home: telecommuting, or as outside consultants or small business people. Once again, no give-and-take conversations take place.

Children no longer go to the park or down to the street corner to find other kids to play with, and they are driven from one organized activity to another.

Communication revolves around responding to the organized situation, rather than being the casual and spontaneous sharing of thoughts, feelings, and experiences.

Although changes in society may bear some responsibility for increasing shyness, shy people tend to blame their discomfort on their own inadequacy, instead of recognizing that they may have had no training in some kinds of interaction, nor any opportunity to rehearse social skills. Perhaps they lacked a good model of a confident adult.

Think of the awkwardness one feels when first confronting the need to comfort a grieving person. What do you say? How do you say it? No one gets lessons in this kind of situation. Shy people may encounter this awkwardness in many social situations that more confident people usually handle with ease.

But when shy people are asked to explain their shyness, they reveal that they believe the reason is some flaw in them, not in early or present experience.

The explanations that shy people come up with for their discomfort may be part of the problem; they emphasize personal inadequacies over which they feel they have no control.

Here's an example of how one shy person tries to understand why she isn't connecting with others: *"I do try to be more socially active. I've been with one group for more than 5 years, and I'm not even close to one of the members! Sometimes I think there is something not right about myself that repels people ... perhaps I'm boring? Speak weird? Look funny?"*

Notice the sad search for explanations within herself, especially that vague *"something not right about myself that repels people."* This kind of explanation doesn't provide any potential solution.

Feelings of Being "Different"

Shy people often think of themselves as "different" from others. Any failure to match the picture of the "ideal" person currently popular in society can bring intense discomfort to the self-conscious, particularly the young. Perceiving yourself as too fat, too thin, too short, too tall, too anything... can provide a ready explanation for feeling unpopular.

> • *When Marcie turned forty, she began to panic because she had not yet found her "ideal" relationship. In a workshop she attended, it suddenly dawned on her that "age" was the current excuse she was using to explain why she didn't connect well with others. In thinking back over her life, she realized that she had blamed her sense of isolation on a variety of reasons: too small breasts in adolescence, an overly large nose in her twenties, and the onset of wrinkles in her thirties. She put blame on everything, in fact, except the real reason: due to childhood disruption and turbulence in her family, she had failed to develop effective social skills.*

A clear look at the real world would demonstrate that a great number of people with paunches, "love handles," outsized features, and sparse hair, who don't meet the current criteria for "attractive," somehow manage to develop warm, loving relationships and supportive families, while we can read about the woes of the excessively attractive in the daily news. Nevertheless, as a nation we remain unconvinced that we can be happy without being physically perfect.

- *Remember Beatrice, the artist who was afraid to display her work? She was the oldest of four children; the others were all blonds with piercing blue eyes, and all of them were larger than she. Bernice was very petite, with very dark hair and green eyes – stunning as an adult. Her relatives all exclaimed over how "different" this child was from the rest of the family.*

  A remark intended to be joking by a relative to her mother, "What, are you raising monkeys now?" convinced her that she was unattractive and unloved.

Chronic Illness and Disability

Any illness, especially chronic illness, which reduces the possibility of full participation in the activities of others, can strike another blow at self-esteem.

Disabilities that are visible, such as blindness, deafness or some physical issues like the inability to walk, produce one kind of discomfort, as other people fail to respond with ease to the disabled person. Disabled people often complain that others fail to make eye contact, or will address them as if they have limited intelligence. Often, people have low expectations for the disabled, keeping them from developing their talents or even basic survival skills, such as traveling to and from school alone. Frequently, clerks, salespeople, and even health care professionals will speak to the caretaker or helper of the disabled person as if the disabled one is mentally incompetent and unable to hold a coherent conversation!

- *Julia, who has been in a wheelchair for decades after an accident, frequently has servers in restaurants ask her companion what she would like to order!*

- *Trish, whose daughter was killed in an auto accident, reported that relatives would ask her husband, in her hearing, how she was "doing." In this case, being in a state of grieving was apparently perceived as a "disability."*

Age as a "disability"

In the United States, age is frequently treated as a disability. A while back, I took my eighty-six-year-old aunt to the eye doctor. A very lively, alert woman who participates vigorously in daily life, she has a wealth of life experience and great sense of humor. After examining her without making any comments (she told me later he had even failed to greet her when he entered the examining room), he came out to the waiting room, and without her permission, started to discuss her case with me. It was necessary to set him straight about which one of us was his patient, and with whom he should be having this discussion. His behavior indicated that he thought she was not capable of holding a meaningful discussion about her current physical state, much less make decisions about the future! And all this because of her age! If he had looked past the stereotype, he would not have seen any other reason why she was not fully competent mentally.

Invisible disabilities

Invisible disabilities, such as a heart condition or Chronic Fatigue Syndrome for example, produce another kind of emotional pain. The person with an invisible disability must face the choice of explaining to others *why* he or she can't participate in a given activity, thus constantly being reminded of the physical difference, or not explain, allowing others to develop their own, sometimes unflattering, explanations for the non-participation.

- *Angela was on disability for severe back pain. Although she appeared healthy (her face was clear and rosy and her expression confident), she could not work or even stand for more than short periods of time. At the supermarket, where she was standing in line with her food stamps in hand, a woman behind her exclaimed to a friend, "Will you look at that! Why, she's just as able-bodied as you and I are, and she's using food stamps!" Angela turned to her and asked, "How is a person in pain supposed to look?"*

Change

A sudden geographical change, without choice or without support, can leave someone vulnerable to feelings of inadequacy.

Consider the difference between an immigrant and a refugee: an immigrant makes the choice to move, and has time to prepare psychologically, physically, and financially. Refugees are forced to move, unwillingly, often having to flee with little more than what they can carry. The move may plunge the refugee, who has already been psychologically battered, into a culture with very different sets of rules and assumptions, and even a new language. It can be hard to remain confident under these circumstances!

Excessive Criticism

Exposure to repeated criticism, especially if it is not balanced with praise, can result in the person believing that the world is a hostile place, which offers little comfort, encouragement, or guidance as to what to do. It only tells you what *not* to do.

Other Traumas

Loss and abandonment

Loss and abandonment, especially in early childhood, through death, divorce, or other reasons, often can lead to insecurity. How much more rejected can you feel than to lose one of the pillars of your life while you are young and vulnerable?

Maxine Harris, Ph.D., author of *The Loss That Is Forever*, describes the effect of the death of a parent in the following way: *"Imagine you are climbing a high mountain through swirling snow. You would be more fearful if it were not for your very experienced guide. Suddenly, your guide disappears, and you are left on the dangerous mountain to proceed alone."*

Neglect

Neglect is also a form of abandonment. Neglect can range from failure to provide the nurturing, shelter, nourishment, and/or health care that children need to grow emotionally.

- *Jenna describes how she was parented in childhood as "janitorially correct": her parents provided a lovely home, good clothing, nutrition, medical care, clothing, and schooling – period. She never remembers receiving any encouragement for her strivings or any comfort for her setbacks. Hugs were not offered. Criticism was plentiful.*

  Jenna became a very strong, dominating person who took charge of situations to ensure that they came out the way she desired. But inside she was still the child who believed she was never good enough for her parents.

Failure to provide clear-cut standards for acceptable behavior is a form of benign neglect, because it fails to give the child any clue as to how to navigate the rough waters of life. Benign neglect may occur either because the parent is too busy and preoccupied to pay attention, or because of fuzzy ideas about permissiveness and self-esteem. The child hasn't been given any help in learning the skills that will help her navigate through life safely, and consequently may have some very unpleasant social experiences.

<u>Abuse and mistreatment</u>

Abuse may be psychological, physical (as in battering), or
sexual. Generally, abusers start with subtle efforts, and then
escalate. The underlying adult-to-child message is: "I am
powerful, and you are not."

Why? Why Me?

When any of the above situations occur, the question
inevitably arises: "Why?" And the next question is: "Why
me?" The answer, irrational though it seems, often is, "I
must somehow have done something to deserve this."

If you don't *know* what it is you have done, or are, that makes
you "deserving" in this manner, then obviously you have no
power to change what you are doing or who you are.

Is Shyness Hereditary?

A fellow teacher of mine once remarked: "I like to tell my
students that shyness is hereditary, because it comforts them
to think that it is not their fault!"

But if shyness is indeed hereditary, what do we do about it?
And how does heredity operate to affect self-esteem?

First, we must distinguish between what is genetic and what
is simply a hereditary predisposition. Your eye color is
genetically determined; there is little you can do to change it.

On the other hand, you can have a hereditary predisposition for diabetes because of your family history, but the lifestyle you choose can make a big difference as to whether you actually develop the disease.

Shyness and low self-esteem are probably behaviors that build on hereditary predispositions or behavioral *tendencies*. To have a tendency for something doesn't mean it is inevitable. For example, we know that certain predispositions that are present at birth tend to remain constant throughout the person's lifespan.

Some Hereditary Predispositions

Activity level

Some infants are, from birth, very active, while others are placid and serene.

- *Charlie, a moving dynamo, was born to older parents who had not planned to have a family. Instead, they had spent years collecting rare glassware, which was displayed on pedestals throughout their home. Charlie's childhood was filled with admonitions: "Charlie, slow down!" "Don't be so boisterous." Charlie's face soon took on an expression of rueful dismay as he attempted, unsuccessfully, to tiptoe through his world.*

  If Charlie had been born into a dynamic family that enjoyed physical sports and loud family discussions in which they playfully disputed each other's ideas, he would have developed a very different level of confidence.

- *Eric loved to play imaginative games with his model toys. He preferred to play with one friend at a time who would accompany him in creating a fantasy situation, which the two would act out. He also liked to sit quietly and read. His parents, avid and active sports fans, were concerned that he wasn't having a "normal" childhood. Eric was labeled "shy."*

Too bad Eric could not have changed places with Charlie! Each would have gotten far more approval and felt more self-confident.

Sensitivity to stimulation

Changes, especially sudden changes, in sound, temperature, and sight, provoke excitement in some infants, distress in some, and little more than curiosity in others. Some infants remain fairly placid in response to sudden changes in stimulation.

According to Harvard researchers and authors of *The Long Shadow of Temperament*, Jerome Kagan and Nancy Snidman, approximately 15 to 20 percent of newborns show increased heart rate, jerky movements, and crying in response to moving mobiles and tape recordings of human voices. Higher heart rates have even been observed in utero in babies later identified as timid.

The same study found that another 15 to 20 percent of babies are described as bold and sociable, *despite* the newness or strangeness of the situation.

We all need time to adjust to change of any kind, which could signal a danger or threat in the environment. Shy people, however, identify situations as threatening that would not bother other people.

For example, Carl Schwartz and others at Harvard Medical School used functional magnetic resonance imaging (fMRI) to examine adults who had been unusually shy in childhood. When these people were shown pictures of unfamiliar faces, they displayed significantly higher activity in the amygdala, a brain structure involved in vigilance and fear, than people who had been unusually outgoing as children.

However, having a "shy brain" doesn't necessarily lead to adult shyness. Environmental factors can play a large role in determining how we manage our fears.

Henderson and Zimbardo report that introverts learn to inhibit behaviors to avoid punishment more quickly than do extroverts, and therefore may learn to avoid and fear cues suggesting those punishing situations may occur.

This physiological or genetic predisposition to inhibition does not develop into shyness 25% of the time. The physiological and/or genetic factors may need to be aggravated by environmental triggers, such as inconsistent or unreliable parenting, insecurity of attachment in the form of difficult relationships with parents, family conflict or chaos, frequent criticism, a dominating older sibling, or a stressful school environment, they report.

We could speculate that children whose nervous systems excite them too much in response to changes would become a little cautious when entering new situations, and be apprehensive about what they might encounter and to what they might have to adapt.

And isn't someone who enters a new situation cautiously and slowly often labeled "shy"? In some situations, this would be intelligent behavior. Perhaps a better word would be "prudent."

One parent may worry about this "shy" child and try to push the child; another may rush to protect the fearful child, while still another may alternately encourage and support the child's entrance into a new, strange environment.

Which is better – a high activity level or a low one? Extreme sensitivity to stimulation or a need to create excitement? It should be obvious that a lot depends on the place one finds oneself: is it accepting or rejecting, rewarding or critical?

If Charlie and Eric had changed places, would the amount of approval that they got for their natural tendencies have changed? It seems likely that Charlie's parents would have accepted Eric as normal, and Eric's parents would have been delighted by Charlie's bounciness.

Many hereditary characteristics can contribute to confidence. Among them are:

- Beauty, which leads to positive experiences with others
- Height: a status symbol in our society
- Good coordination, which can lead to being a successful athlete

Yet, looking around the world, you can find numerous examples of people who do not meet today's standards for "beauty," yet they are loved and successful in many ways. Talent, hard work, and the ability to connect meaningfully with others can overcome any physical status symbol that society sets up.

The External Environment

The "environment" consists of many things, including other people and their reactions. One of the negative aspects of the long period of development that humans experience is that we are helpless and at the mercy of others when we are young. Therefore, we pay close attention to what they tell us about ourselves. It is reflected in their behavior and in their eyes. Part of becoming mature is to seek information from different sources – and to evaluate it carefully. As already noted, people with low self-esteem are likely to be more sensitive to the reactions of others than is healthy for them.

Here are some of the ways people have impact on our self-concept:

They *observe* us: our appearance, natural tendencies, and desires, and *judge* whether or not they approve. They then *reward* us for behaviors they like and *withhold* rewards for those they don't like. They may actively *discourage* our natural tendencies, for example to be vigorously active or to create lots of stimulation in our environment.

They may give us *cues* telling us that they have developed certain *expectations* for us. For example, they may say such things as:

> "Let Josh handle it. He's such a diplomat."
> "Oh, good, Andrea's here. She's always good with this kind of problem."

Or they may turn expectantly, looking relieved when Andrea enters the room or when Josh speaks up. If David is also a low-key, quiet person who solves problems, these qualities may be overlooked as Andrea has already established herself in that role.

The Internal Environment

Beliefs, labels, and roles

Even if we move out of our environment, we retain beliefs about ourselves that were formed in that environment. These beliefs remain fairly constant despite external changes. Some of these beliefs can be thought of as *labels* that got pasted on us one day:

- *Richard's mother, although she loved him dearly, referred to him laughingly as clumsy. She didn't remember that it had started one winter when he had a cold. All she knew was that she could expect him to drop or bump into things regularly. She didn't remember that all toddlers can be very clumsy, nor that it started when he had a fever. She didn't realize that she became alert to any incidence of clumsiness on his part. Behavior that she once would have accepted as being a part of normal child development had become a trait, which Richard was doomed to carry with him for a very long time.*

  In a discussion about labels, Richard suddenly said he had just realized that he actually tried to do something clumsy when he entered a new situation! Why would anyone try to do something that is embarrassing? Because he was so sure he would do it anyway, he felt a great need to get the embarrassing episode over with!

- *Chad had always been seen as somewhat "slow" in comparison to his brothers and sisters. Chad was extremely large for his age and was a victim of "size-age" confusion. Because he was large, he looked several years older than he actually was, and was therefore judged in comparison to those older children. In this comparison, he appeared to be somewhat uncoordinated and slow mentally. This evaluation of Chad continued even though he brought home school reports and papers on which the grades exceeded those of his brothers and sisters. Upon* reflection, Chad's older sister remarked that actually Chad had done better than any of his siblings in school.

Labels can be thought of as long-standing judgments that are:
- Based on limited observation(s);
- Applicable long term;
- Apt to ignore contradictory evidence;
- Likely to trigger arguments to support the label; and
- Toxic when the person being labeled buys into the label.

These labels may also be applied to others, but they are often accepted without questioning by the person to whom they are applied, even when contradictory evidence exists.

- *Stephie knew she was a poor athlete. She had been the last team member chosen in every game she played. Physical education classes were a nightmare for her, as she repeatedly missed balls, to the jeers of her classmates.*

  One day the teacher announced that the game for the day was volleyball, and Stephie was to serve first. Everyone (predictably) groaned. Stephie served the ball right over the net, where it fell at the feet of the surprised players. She served a second time, dropping the ball in a different place on the other team's court. She, in fact, served twenty-one times without the other team being able to return the ball.

The other players left the gym grumbling at the fact that a poor player had once again ruined the game for them!

Twenty years later, Stephie found that she suffered from poor visual tracking, and therefore had great difficulty hitting a moving object. But when the object stood still, as it did when she served the volleyball, she was deadly accurate. Only then did she question the label given to her so long ago: poor athlete.

We see again that, once a label is given, no one looks at the evidence that suggests the label is not accurate.

Nicknames may be flattering or unflattering labels. They attempt to sum up some quality that is apparent to the person bestowing the nickname. They may be given in jest, or seriously, as a true description of the person.

The mother who called one daughter "Princess" may have felt loving, but she also may have set up for her unreal expectations about what reactions to expect from others. And the mother never noticed the dismal expression on her other daughter's face when she used this flattering nickname.

This author's childhood nickname was, briefly, "Nutsy," and this was given by a loving family member who meant no harm, possibly in response to the fact that I liked to clown. I remember turning fiercely on my family when I started school, terrified my schoolmates would find out and tease me.

Shyness as a label

The word "shy" in itself is a label. It often gets applied, inaccurately, to people who are good listeners, introverts, or just intelligent enough to be quiet in a new situation until they grasp what is going on, as well as to people who do have some social anxiety.

It is not a positive label. The effect on the person who is being so labeled can be devastating. Parents may publicly explain a child's reluctance to enter a new situation or speak up with the words, "(S)he's a little shy." The child has just learned something about him- or herself, and it is not positive.

How much better it would be to say, "(S)he is just learning how to greet people – or to enter new situations."

Overcoming the anxiety of shyness involves taking risks. Someone who is a little hesitant about social situations may be braced to take some action to be included, which could result in a positive outcome – friendliness, approval and a growth experience. But if someone comments on that person's shyness, instead of it being a reward, the person may find that his or her "disability" is being publicly announced.

To the truly shy, this can feel like walking across a room stark naked in front of rows of jeering people.

Roles can be thought of as clusters of behaviors that are considered to be appropriate to a given category. If you are in a certain category, then you have a mental list of appropriate characteristics. We all learn the rules of our particular culture very early, such as: "Big boys don't cry," or "Girls aren't good at math."

- *Esther was fortunate in being able to buy a lovely but run-down home. She didn't have enough money to hire someone to fix it up, however. So she lived for years in dingy rooms with old, discolored wallpaper hanging from the walls in strips. She could have found information on how to do some painting and refurbishing herself, but "Women don't <u>do</u> work like that," she explained.*

The danger in role-playing lies in behaving in ways that really aren't necessary or comfortable, or in denying yourself activities or attitudes because of limited beliefs about the requirements of the role.

The environment supports who we are, as people around us have expectations for us based on their interaction with us. They give us signals to indicate how they expect us to behave, and reward or punish us for our behavior. When environmental support is withdrawn (for example, when we move away from a familiar group and setting) the effect can quickly arouse anxiety.

This anxiety that may be aroused when we leave our "home" environment is called homesickness. A more severe form of homesickness is known as culture shock.

Environmental change, and other people's faulty perceptions, may in fact have helped to cause the problem, but only the individual can solve it for him- or herself.

The following chart shows these factors as they contribute to the development of self-concept, and therefore to self-esteem.

The Development of Self-Esteem

Heredity +	**Environment** +	**Beliefs**
Hereditary predispositions:	Rewards	Beliefs about self
Sensitivity to stimulation	Punishment	Labels
Activity level	Cues	May be based on limited observations
	Expectations	Long lasting
	Models	Ignore conflicting evidence
	Opportunities provided (or not)	Accepted by labeler & labelee
	Resistance to change	Roles: include gender,
	Pressure to preserve status quo	socioeconomic status, age, ethnicity, religion, profession

A Program for Change

Suppose you decide you want to change. Even if others say they want you to change, you may be surprised to find that those people don't always give you support.

Althea's friends and family have urged her for years to be more outgoing and to let others know about her great sense of humor. Althea has resisted until this year, when she finally has decided she would like her good qualities to be recognized by others. Quietly, she devises a program for change that includes:

- Changing her appearance, with a new haircut and different selection of clothing (as a signal to herself and others that a new regime was starting).
- Becoming well-informed on current events in order to be able to hold knowledgeable conversations with others. (Shy people are often so wrapped up in themselves they miss what is going on in the world, or are hesitant to speak up for fear of being wrong.)
- Taking a course in learning new conversational skills.
- Selecting a hobby, something she could excel at, and about which she could speak with authority.
- Observing a role model – someone she admires who seems to be very much at ease in social situations.

Are Althea's friends and family delighted when they observe these changes? Maybe – and maybe not.

People who advise others to change overlook the fact that we live in a social network. If one person changes, so must others in the network. The result may be that Althea encounters *resistance to change* and pressure to *return to the status quo*.

If Althea becomes an animated conversationalist, someone else in her group may have to relinquish their time talking in order to yield the floor to her. If she develops a deep interest in modern art or hockey and talks knowledgably about it, someone else may feel his expertise has been undermined. If the competition is too keen, and the derogation of her new skills too great, she may retreat again into shyness.

Althea might have a better chance if she went to another town and introduced herself to new people the way she wants to be perceived. No one will think that she is "not herself" when she acts outgoing, because they have no basis for comparison.

In the following chapters, you will find skills that will help you to enlist people as supporters in your quest for a happier life, including the most important skill of all, risk-taking.

Action steps for Chapter 2:

These exercises are designed, as were the exercises at the end of Chapter 1, to take the focus off yourself and start looking outward more often.

1. This week, notice something positive that each person you meet does: holds the door for you, smiles, says or does something kind, shows or talks about important qualities such as kindness to others, goes out of the way to be helpful in giving you directions, provides extra service in a store, greets others with enthusiasm.

2. Start keeping a log of all the positive actions you have noticed. Think of them as potential models for your own behavior.

3. How does your environment (people around you, activities you engage in) contribute to your identity and to your present level of self-esteem?

Chapter 3:
Feeling Bad Is Just the Start:
Consequences of Shyness/Low Self-Esteem

Most people, when asked about what shyness feels like, report extreme discomfort in social situations when they become the center of someone else's attention. They're even embarrassed about blushing because they had felt uncomfortable! Other shy people may mention a tendency to perspire, especially if they have to shake hands with someone (and their hands are wet).

Digging deeper, they may remark on the sense of isolation, depression, and overall unhappiness.

But there are more consequences:

Lower Level of Success

For every talented and successful person you see in any field, there are tens, sometimes hundreds, and in some cases, thousands of people who are similarly or even more talented and skilled. You will never hear their voices, nor see them, for they lack the psychological skills – the confidence and social abilities – that would allow them to connect with others, and uncover the opportunities where they could display their talents.

Charles Garfield, author of the Peak Performance studies, states that, "Peak Performers don't do it alone." They build a network of supporting people – something shy and low self-esteem people have difficulty doing.

The lowered visibility of shy people, due to their lack of conversational and social skills, may lead to fewer employment opportunities or promotions.

Poor Evaluations from Others

Other people tend to see shy people as less intelligent, less competent, and less attractive. And shy people fuel this fire with their own behavior.

- *Tracy was frustrated. Loaded with good ideas, she was timid about expressing them at meetings of her work group, for fear of possible ridicule. Often she whispered her contribution in a low voice, only to have one of her co-workers take it up loudly with the full group. The result? The group thought the co-worker was a genius! Tracy had not received credit for her good ideas for years, dating back to her school days.*

And it follows that shy people make less money than non-shy people, not only because of lower evaluations, but perhaps because they are afraid to ask for more money.

Attack from Without and Within

Shy people punish themselves enough by perseverating over and focusing on their supposed "failures." But punishment doesn't always come from within.

The publicly shy *look* shy, showing many of the characteristics listed above, while the privately shy (also known as the Shy Extrovert) may show surface social skills, but somehow miss that essential warm connection with others, and therefore they may be judged as aloof, cold, and even arrogant.

Many performers, who look supremely confident while performing, may appear aloof and arrogant when fans encounter them offstage. In fact, they are often privately shy.

The problem for the privately shy is that others may want to attack what they perceive as arrogance. So, the downside of looking confident without developing the skills to connect with other people may then be that others treat you more severely because they want to "take you down a peg." In other words, people with low self-esteem may feel that the world is a harsh and lonely place in which they inexplicably encounter more rejection than others, and this may be an accurate picture of what the person has actually experienced.

Other ways in which a privately shy person copes may be by acting as the group "clown." Some people even project surface "bluster": forceful speaking voice, aggressive body language, and strong initiation of behavior.

What are the clues that might tell you that this "self-confident" person is really insecure?

- *Chloe was an extremely charming and assertive, even aggressive woman. When she entered any new environment, she immediately "took charge." She was very critical of others, judging them for small flaws in dress or speech that deviated from what she considered to be her high standards.*

  Those who were closer to her, however, knew that when someone called one of her mistakes to her attention, she immediately began to punish herself, saying such things as "Stupid me! How could I have done that! I'm a walking disaster."

Poor Health

Low self-esteem and shyness can lead one to avoid social situations, and social isolation has an impact on the immune system. Isolated people are more likely to become ill, and die at an earlier age than do those who are warmly connected to family and friends. In August 2009, a study published by the American Psychosomatic Society found that there was a direct correlation between loneliness and coronary heart disease.

There are a number of reasons why social isolation would contribute to poor health.

- People who are connected to others may have more regular schedules for eating and sleeping. People close to them may urge them to get medical exams, quit smoking, exercise more regularly, or eat better.

- Shy people may be reluctant to discuss sensitive problems with doctors and other caregivers.

- Poorer job success may lead to lower income, including lower poorer medical care.

- And of course, there is the emotional toll of persistent anxiety and/or depression.

"Alone" is not the same as "lonely"

"Alone" is not the same as "lonely" and the introvert's preference for a smaller social circle should not be confused with social isolation.

However, people have different tolerance levels for stimulation, including social stimulation. Some people need to have constant social interaction; others require time alone in order to reflect upon their thoughts and to relax. In fact, Abraham Maslow, in his Hierarchy of Needs theory of human motivation, includes a desire to spend some time alone as one of the characteristics of "self-actualization," a high state of development in which the self-actualized person is self-aware, self-accepting, socially responsive, creative, spontaneous, and open to new experiences.

To be lonely is to feel isolated, to experience anxiety over the experience of being alone, and to believe that there is a more desirable situation one is missing. It is possible to be lonely in the middle of a crowd.

The Fight-or-Flight Response

Many of the symptoms of shyness – rapid heartbeat, excessive perspiration, muscular tension, tremors – are symptoms of the fight-or-flight response, the response that evolved to save our lives when physically threatened. These changes gave our ancestors the speed to escape predators or the strength to compete for food.

But nowadays the response is most often activated in social situations, where neither strength nor speed is required. Instead, clear thinking and cool action are needed.

The shy person experiences the fight-or-flight response more often than the non-shy – often on a daily basis. In terms of health, this means that the body is frequently subjected to the unnecessary wear-and-tear of a rapidly pounding heart and a rise in blood pressure. Furthermore, chronic stress, as experienced by the chronically shy, can lead to chronically high levels of cortisol, a hormone that regulates inflammation. As Sheldon Cohen and a team at Carnegie Mellon University found, the cells of the immune system become insensitive to cortisol and to hormonal control, producing high levels of inflammation that promote disease such as cardiac disease, asthma, and autoimmune disorders.

Being Misunderstood

Someone doesn't understand you, and you give up rather than face what you perceive as the hopeless task of explaining yourself. The other person sees you as stupid, while you feel frustrated.

- *Darrell was a little nervous on the first day of his new job, so when another employee, who had worked there longer, addressed him as "Donald," he didn't correct him. He was too insecure on the second, third, and following days to make the correction. A year and a half later, he had still not told his co-worker his correct name, and the co-worker was still calling him Donald. Even a very confident person might feel a little foolish to make the change at that point, but a very confident person wouldn't have gotten into this dilemma in the first place.*

  Darrell was too unsure of himself even to make sure others knew his real name, much less any other information that would have defined him as an individual.

Is Self-Esteem about "Feeling Good"?

Self-esteem is not about *feeling good* because you are loved, attractive, have a fulfilling profession or a secure life style. If these are the bases for your self-esteem, you are extremely vulnerable, because any one of them can be snatched away in a moment. A loved one steps off the curb at the wrong moment, you suffer an accident which doesn't allow you to continue your life's work, a major disaster robs you of your life's savings – any of these events, or others, could remove your basis for well-being in a instant.

Self-esteem is about *doing well* – developing the skills that can affect the course of your life. More importantly, it is about knowing that you *can* handle whatever comes your way.

A colleague of mine told me this story about her daughter:

- *The daughter came home in tears every day from her fifth grade class. Her relationship with her new teacher was poor; nothing she did seemed to be right, and the teacher frequently and sarcastically commented on the quality of her work and her personal work habits.*

  By all accounts, the situation seemed to be an unfair one, and my friend said to her daughter, "If you like, I will go to school and talk to the principal about switching you to another class. Or, we can work together so that you learn how to deal with difficult people. It's your choice." And the daughter chose to stay, and with the help of her wise mother, learn to handle this kind of difficult situation.

  Although the daughter probably experienced some anxiety, anger, and depression during the school year, she also experienced a sense of mastery and acquired skills that she would use many times in the years to come. She learned not to be so devastated by one person's disapproval, how to use the support of others to get through a difficult period in life, even how to see things from another person's (the teacher's) point of view.

If the daughter had chosen option number one, to be removed from the painful classroom situation, she would have felt immediately better. But in the long run, she would have been a weaker and more vulnerable person, whose major response to difficulty was to flee.

Learning to love again after a loss, finding a new career path when one is closed, getting back on your feet after financial disaster, discovering that, if your appearance is altered, you have behaviors that are attractive to others, all depend upon the development of life skills, and the recognition that you have those skills. "Feeling good" is a by-product of success in solving life's problems.

The payoff for developing good self-esteem is tremendous:
- A wealth of supportive relationships, both personal and professional
- A decreased need to defend yourself against psychological onslaughts by others
- Improved health
- And most of all, the feeling that you are participating joyously in life, allowing your talents to unfold and sharing that joy with others

The process of developing high self-esteem is not without stress. My friend's daughter displayed a willingness to take small, daily risks, but in doing so, she gradually expanded her "comfort zone."

"Only those who will risk going too far can possibly know how far they can go."~ T.S. Eliot

Action steps for Chapter 3:

1. What have been some of the consequences of shyness and low self-esteem in your life?

2. List some of the skills and competencies in your life of which you are proud. Show your list to someone who knows you well and ask them to add to it.

3. Think back over times when you feel you have been lucky or unlucky in your life. Can you now see how your skills – social, artistic, technical, etc. – or lack of them might have been responsible?

Chapter 4:

Discover How Others Misunderstand You

Why they don't understand you ~ and how you misunderstand them
Includes discovering how you misunderstand yourself ~ or let yourself be
misunderstood

"For as far back as I can recall," said Aretha, who was shy, "I was afraid to meet new kids, go to parties, speak up in public. I desperately wanted to be normal like other kids. My parents and my teachers often commented on how I was 'different.' Although they said it warmly, I'm not sure it was a compliment."

What is "Normal"?

Parents want their children to be normal, teachers may want their students to be normal, and even people who are different may wish that they were normal. Where do they get their pictures of what constitutes "normal"? Probably from their own background and the expectations they have developed. One common expectation is that our own goals, hopes, wants and fears are widespread and shared with others. Another expectation is that everyone will communicate these goals, hopes, wants and fears in a similar language and style.

Nothing could be farther from the truth.

> It is impossible
> For someone else
> To betray you
>
> The illusion of betrayal can occur
> Only if you have expectations
> Of others being a certain way
> And then they are different
>
> ~Peter Rengel, in *Seeds of Light*

The Emotions of Normal People: Four Different Patterns of Normal Behavior

William Moulton Marston, in 1928, addressed this question in *Emotions of Normal People*. He proposed that "normal" behavior comes in different patterns: in fact, four patterns which are distinct from one another, yet all are potentially adaptive and useful.

People do things for their own reasons, not yours

Marston suggested that one major factor that distinguishes people is their "focus": what they consider to be important. Out of the many experiences we have, we tend to pay attention to the things we feel are important, and filter out many "unnecessary" details.

For instance, one person may be so focused on a goal that she ignores seemingly trivial information, such as the disapproval of others or the emotional needs and responses of others. Another person, in the same environment, may notice slight changes in body language or tone of voice on the part of others, and be eager to adjust his or her communication to the needs of that person. Two people can be in the same room, experiencing the same events, but electing to pay attention to different aspects of that experience, filtering out the things that don't fit his or her focus.

Another issue is that of safety. Someone once asked Albert Einstein, "What is the most important question in the universe?" He thought a moment and answered, "The most important question is this: Is the universe a safe place or an unsafe place? *Because no matter what answer you come up with, you will always find the evidence to support it!*"

One of the many benefits of studying these different behavioral styles is to understand why other people may misunderstand you, and what you can do, easily and gracefully, to make sure that they do understand you.

As we saw in "The Vicious Circle" in Chapter 1, beliefs about ourselves become actions, which trigger feedback from others, often confirming our beliefs. Studying the many motives other people can have for doing what they do can help minimize the self-conscious belief that other people are doing things to us, or because of us.

They are doing what they do for their own reasons!

Understanding the behavioral styles can also provide different "windows" on the world through which to see behavior. We can then learn to feel safer and to become more accepting of the individual differences that enrich life.

In this chapter, we will look at different types of behavioral styles that people adopt, their motivations, fears, and the ways they handle them. By studying these different types of behavior, it is possible, for example, to learn how to have an explanation for other people's actions that is not too self-referent. Each may be thinking that this is the best possible way to behave in the current situation, even if you think otherwise.

<u>Examples</u>

- *Mark first saw Kathy in a night class he was attending. She was very attractive, and as he looked at her, she made eye contact with him and smiled. The next time the class met, students were asked to sit at lab tables, and she drifted towards his table. After class, she lingered to talk as the other students left. This went on for several classes, as Mark debated whether or not she was attracted to him, and would accept an invitation to go out. Just as he made up his mind that it was safe to ask her for a date, her behavior changed abruptly. She entered the next class dressed in a stylish, even sexy, outfit, swept past him without a greeting and took a seat at another lab table with another male (but within Mark's sight), where she chatted animatedly with her new partner.*

This behavior continued for the rest of the semester.

Mark's long-standing belief that women were impossible to understand was confirmed. So was Kathy's belief that she could never have a rewarding relationship.

***

- *Jack left the engineering firm with which he was associated to start his own business with Jim, who had been a co-worker in the same firm. Initially, they both had the same vision and enthusiasm, working long hours with good humor to get their business started. As time went on, however, Jack became more and more expansive. He wanted to bring more and more people into the company, open branch offices, and take on new projects that were different in focus from what they had originally planned. Furthermore, he became more and more sociable, pressuring Jim to join him in playing golf, sailing, and just generally hanging around with a large group of friendly people.*

  Jim, on the other hand, was interested in proceeding slowly and doing in-depth research before he made any changes in the business plan. He warmed up to new people slowly, and liked to survey them cautiously before getting too deeply involved. Jim also liked, and needed, to spend some time by himself every day.

Jack tried to persuade him that too much perfectionism was holding back the business, and was, furthermore, unhealthy. So was Jim's unsociable behavior, according to Jack, although he hadn't noticed it when their relationship began.

The partnership didn't last, nor did Jack and Jim's friendship. Each thought the other was a little "peculiar."

***

- *When Andrea met Russ, she was warmed and excited by his buoyant "take charge" manner. Coming from a quiet, non-assertive background, she found she felt "safe" in new situations when she was with Russ. When they entered a luxurious restaurant, he confidently requested (and got) the lovely window seat that she secretly preferred, but would never have asked for by herself. In fact, he usually asked for, and got, what he wanted. He was quite a change from her quiet, submissive father, who simply accepted with good grace what was given to him.*

  Russ was charmed by Andrea's even-tempered warmth and her tolerance of his often swift swings of mood from buoyant to irritated. He felt comforted by the fact that he could always count on her to be soothing and calm. So he was stunned when, after several years of marriage, she suddenly erupted stormily, accusing him of being domineering and insensitive. Furthermore, she then "clammed up" and refused to discuss the issue anymore. He was bewildered, she felt shaken and guilty, and the distance between them grew.

***

How did these relationships go so wrong? That is one of the questions to be answered in this chapter.

In order to avoid being misunderstood by others, it is important to understand yourself and what makes you different – normally – from those others.

Marston's work resulted in the development of theories of human behavior based on four clusters of characteristics. In the 1970's Dr. John Geier developed a psychological inventory called the *Personal Profile System®* with which to determine how much of each of these characteristics one possesses, and verified that there are four different clusters of normal behavioral traits, or styles. These four clusters, or styles, are Dominance, Influence, Steadiness, and Conscientiousness (D, I, S and C for short).

(The *Personal Profile System* is now called *DiSC® Classic*, and is published by Inscape Publishing. It has been used by more than 40 million people worldwide to improve communication, ease frustration and conflict, and develop effective managers and teams.)

You may feel that you seem to be several of these styles, at different times, and you would be quite right. Most people are not an "undiluted" style; instead, individuals tend to possess some of each of the styles. We differ in the extent that each of these styles plays in our particular personality.

However, in discussing these behavioral styles, for shorthand, we will refer to people by their primary characteristic, with a shorthand description of each characteristic.

For example, we may say "High D" or "Low S" to describe where someone falls on the scale.

Different "Languages" Within One Language

We've already indicated that different behavioral styles tend to focus on different things as being of major importance, but what people tend to focus on can be revealed by the way they choose to communicate.

Within a spoken language there can be many forms of communication: two of these are direct communication and indirect communication. Misunderstandings can often arise because two speakers of the same language are using different styles, so different that they are puzzling or even angering one another.

The following is a thumbnail view of each style and its patterns of behavior:

Dominance

People who score high in **Dominance** are, at their best, determined and pioneering. This style involves control, power, and assertiveness. Dominant people don't let obstacles get in their way and they make decisions quickly.

If a Dominant experiences shyness at all, it is well-masked private shyness. Shy High D's can experience sensations of isolation and loneliness even when they are being forceful leaders. It is likely that many "shy extroverts" fall into this category.

Focus: The focus of this style is on getting a task done, on winning the goal. Their other behaviors then reflect this focus.

Communication style: Direct. Their communications about what they want, or like or don't like, are clear and direct, *and they expect the same communication style from others.* D's have no difficulty speaking up, asking for what they want, and expressing displeasure. They do this quickly, because they are often impatient to reach a goal, for which the communication is one of the stepping stones.

They expect others to do the same, and when they don't, the D assumes that person doesn't care very much one way or another.

Misunderstands: It follows that the D is mystified by others who do not speak up for themselves.

Fears and is stressed by: If taking charge in order to reach a goal is the focus, then being out of control of a situation is extremely threatening to this style.

Most often misunderstood by others because of: Competitiveness and forceful speaking style, which may be interpreted as forceful, aggressive, even bullying.

Strengths they bring to a situation: Take-charge leadership in emergency situations, or other situations where the need for a decision is strong, but others are unwilling or unable to make one.

When the strengths become a liability: D's often see competitions where others do not: for example, cutting in and out of traffic to gain the advantage of a few seconds in reaching a goal.

When under stress, a Dominant is likely to dismiss information that might suggest that slowing down is a good idea.

Handles stress by: Engaging in vigorous physical activity.

Influence

Influencers are warm, animated, persuasive and optimistic. Interested in social situations, they enjoy being the center of attention, and are often great motivational leaders.

I's, like the D's, may be performers masking an underlying insecurity, and are also candidates for being "shy extroverts." At their best, they are charming and engaging. Taking center stage and motivating others to feel good comes naturally to them.

Focus: To be liked and admired by others.

Communication style: Direct. Excellent communicators, they speak openly about their emotional responses to life, and *expect others to be equally open.* They can easily talk about their feelings and other aspects of their personal lives. They may pressure others to reveal personal information, too, and feel rejected when they don't. They are also great at speaking enthusiastically and even passionately in an effort to convince others, and often put a positive spin on their discussions.

They communicate this way because they have a strong need to be close to others, and to be perceived in a positive light.

They are usually more direct when it comes to expressing positive feelings and establishing relationships, but less direct when it comes to expressing anger or criticizing others.

Misunderstands: People who don't enjoy being center stage, participating in social situations, or talking about their personal feelings. The need for quiet and for space on the part of the introvert (as represented most often by the next two styles we will consider), can be puzzling to them and they may continually ask, "Are you sure you're OK? Can I get/do anything for you?"

Fears and is stressed by: Because they are used to taking center stage, they feel personal rejection keenly. This can include feeling pushed to the side by someone else's prominence in a group.

Most often misunderstood by others because of: Intensity of emotional communication, trying to get close to others too fast. The enthusiasm and zest with which they express their ideas and world views may leave others thinking they're a little delusional or self-aggrandizing.

Strengths: People who have a lot of this quality make inspiring leaders, motivating and energizing others with their enthusiasm.

When strengths become a liability: The great need to be liked by others may lead to great unwillingness to offend others, and therefore to indecision.

In an effort to be liked by everyone, the I may say what others want to hear. What the I says to Person A ("I think you have proposed a great plan") may contradict what is said to Person B ("I don't think A's plan is very sound"), leaving the I sometimes looking dishonest and even manipulative.

Handles stress by: Getting together with others and doing something sociable, such as going dancing.

Steadiness

Steadiness people show patience, persistence and

68

thoughtfulness, and are great in groups. They are easy to be around, appearing calm and relaxed. They enjoy being part of a harmonious team.

People who are high in this characteristic may be perceived as shy in an environment where extroverted behavior is expected, and being labeled as "shy" can increase feelings of social anxiety even when those feelings were low to non-existent initially.

Focus: The focus of the S is to be a part of a supportive group of people who work and socialize well together.

Communication style: Indirect. They think of themselves as tactful and diplomatic. Their communication style at its best is very agreeable; *they dislike openly argumentative conversation.* Since they enjoy being part of a group, an S may honestly prefer to have group consensus about something as simple as where to go to lunch, rather than insist on his or her preference.

Misunderstands: Extremely outgoing behavior, whether it is the assertive behavior of the D or the spontaneous social behavior of the I, and especially behavior that is considered by the S to be "noisy" or even "rowdy."

Fears and is stressed by: Too much noise of any kind can be too much stimulation for the S. They dislike conflict, sometimes so strongly that they don't even want to be in the vicinity of raised, argumentative voices, even when those voices are not directed at them, but are part of a play or movie.

Most often misunderstood by: The indirect style of communication leaves them vulnerable to being "run over" by other, more direct communicators. For example, two S's may hold the following conversation:

Person A: "Are you getting hungry?"

Person B: "A little bit. Are you?"

Person A: "Yes, a little. Where would you like to go?"

Person B: "Oh, I don't know. Do you like Chinese?"

Actually, they may quickly and smoothly – to their satisfaction – reach an agreement and proceed.

But trying this technique with a direct communicator may turn out very differently, as in this example:

Person A (an S): "Are you getting hungry?"

Person B (a D): "No."

The indirect communicator may try other indirect comments to express his or her needs, but the direct communicator may miss all the clues and continue on, leaving the indirect communicator puzzled and resentful.

Strengths: The typically stable temperament of the S, together with the habit of following through on commitments, makes this kind of person very valuable in both personal relationships and on work teams.

Strengths become a liability when: The S, in an attempt to avoid conflict, "clams up" when asked his or her position. At some point, having suppressed feelings and thoughts for some time, the S is likely to blow up, surprising everyone who has experienced this person as calm and patient.

Handles stress by: Takes a quiet time-out from everything and everybody. Their preferred method of handling conflict is often to take flight rather than face the issue.

Conscientiousness

C's are conscientious, detail-oriented, and concerned with structure and organization. They pride themselves on the high quality of their precise work. They dislike being wrong, and their careful diplomatic communication style reflects this.

People with high carefulness characteristics are, like the S, more likely to be perceived and labeled as shy. In turn, they become socially uncomfortable at being somehow regarded as "abnormal."

Focus: They often pride themselves on doing careful, high-quality work in any area of life.

Communication style: Indirect. They are diplomatic, and choose their words carefully in order to avoid making a mistake. Because they are careful about facts, they tend to dismiss what they believe is overly emotional communication as being designed to manipulate rather than inform.

Misunderstands: The spontaneous social behavior and often impassioned communication style of the I as being emotionally manipulative. Thinks of the quick, decisive behavior of the D as being unnecessarily risky.

Fears and is stressed by: Being rushed, whether it is in a work project or in a relationship; not being allowed to pursue perfectionism. Questioning the accuracy of his/her work or facts is very stressful to this extremely careful person.

Most often misunderstood by: A great need for privacy, which is misinterpreted as being anti-social. In fact, they simply desire less social activity than many others, and prefer one-on-one encounters.

When others talk to a C about an emotional issue, such as a conflict, the C will ask careful questions to get at the facts, leading the more emotional speaker to feel that the C is disbelieving the story. Not so; the C simply wants all the facts before feeling safe enough to give an opinion or make a decision.

Strengths: The focus on fact-gathering and precision is of vital importance in many areas of life, whether it be finances, construction, or other areas in which exact planning is needed.

When strengths become a liability: Focusing on facts to the exclusion of feelings in personal relationships can be a mistake in these areas where there often are no hard and fixed facts. This tendency can alienate others, and eventually leave the C unsatisfied in those areas of life.

Handles stress by: Withdrawal, with a focus on an all-consuming activity that involves precision and concentration.

Can these behavioral differences ever be resolved? People with all of these styles can learn to be more comfortable with other people.

Let's go back and analyze the examples at the beginning of this chapter.

Mark and Cathy: Mark, a C, was doing his usual job of collecting sufficient data before making a move. Cathy, an I, was displaying her enthusiasm for Mark, and assuming that they were connecting far faster than he was comfortable with. Their relationship might have worked if she had recognized his behavioral style and been willing to slow down a little, or if he had been able to take the small risk of asking her for coffee after class "to discuss the class."

Can a relationship between two such different behavioral styles work? Yes, if they are willing to give a little, and to appreciate (and express that appreciation about) the differences between them. Then they might have found that Mark valued her enthusiasm and optimism, and that Cathy enjoyed the solidity of Mark's approach to life.

Jim and Jack: Here we see another example of a conflict between an I and a C, this time in a business setting. Jim's persistent insistence that Jack be more sociable led Jack to withdraw, feeling confused and a little hurt, and leaving Jim without the more solid grounded approach of his partner, which would have kept him from making some of the big business mistakes his enthusiastic optimism led him into.

Andrea and Russ: This is an example of a conflicted relationship between a D, Russ, and an S, Andrea. This was a true case of opposites attracting: he loved her for her calmness and emotional stability (and eventually became irritated by it); she was thrilled by his decisive take-charge manner, which allowed her to retreat from conflict while he handled it (but then she felt overwhelmed by it).

This relationship was definitely worth saving, if Andrea had taken some assertiveness training so that Russ knew what the heck she really wanted (or didn't want), and if Russ had learned to tone down his decisive, dominant tone of voice and become a better listener in Andrea's presence.

So here's a list of things that each behavioral style needs to learn in order to be less misunderstood by others:

The D needs to learn how to help other people feel safe in the D's presence, by speaking a little less loudly, and by using a little less intimidating body language, such as standing over someone while giving them negative feedback.

Intimidating communication leads others to withhold information that may be vital, because the bearer of the news is afraid of the negative reaction he or she may trigger.

The I needs to learn to turn the spotlight on others, too, in order to share the approval. Noticing excellent qualities in others and commenting on them is a great way to build a network of friends and supporters.

I's can also learn to be assertive, even when fearing others will disapprove and not like them for it. People will, in the long run, like you better if you are just calmly honest with them.

The S can benefit from perceiving that forceful people are not as threatening as they appear, and that assertive communication will more likely be respected, not rejected. Learn to ask directly for what you want, don't expect people to guess from what you believe to be subtle and diplomatic comments, and above all, don't blame others if they don't get your indirect communication. They're not being selfish or rude; it's simply a language they don't understand. In fact, they don't even hear it; it just becomes background noise, as far as they are concerned.

The C may need to deal with overuse of perfectionism, which not only handicaps the C but also threatens others because of its critical nature. (A perfectionist is assumed by others to be turning the same critical spotlight on others as on themselves.)

C's also need to understand that providing a lengthy, detailed prelude on a topic to an impatient and decisive person, such as a D or an I, isn't necessary and may trigger an irritated response.

Who's in Charge? Which One is the Better Leader?

Many people, particularly in the United States, assume that the High D, with his/her directive, decisive, assertive style is the ideal leader. A second candidate would be the I, who can take over a whole roomful of people with charm.

They may be great leaders, under certain circumstances. High D people perform particularly well under pressure, such as in emergency rooms of hospitals, where they must take charge and make quick decisions, or in high-stakes athletic competitions, where a High D delights in the challenge of competition that might feel threatening to another.

- *Mary, a high I and a travel and events planner, was superb at her job. She could meet a weary group of travelers and with her bright, optimistic, conversational style, have them laughing and energized within minutes. A master of the "soft touch," she could get them, through her verbal skill and use of humor, to accept a change of plans that they might have stubbornly resisted if she had simply told them directly that the change was happening and there was nothing they could do about it.*

Sometimes groups need an enthusiastic motivator more than they need no-nonsense information.

But the definition of a leader is someone who others are willing to follow. A leader without followers is not a leader.

The drawback of the D is that their direct, challenging style may discourage followers, rather than encourage them.

The I may draw followers because of the high-energy charm they project, but it is important for the I to learn to recognize and validate the contributions of the followers rather than hug all of the attention.

The definition of a good leader should rest, not just on the personality of the leader, but also on the goal of the group being led.

For example, here's a leadership style that often goes unrecognized:

- *Ruth is a lovely gentle person and, as an S, she is a good non-judgmental listener. She loves to create a harmonious atmosphere for herself and others, and as a facilitator of a support group for cardiac patients she does just that. Participants arrive to find a room filled with fresh flowers and little candles placed in corners to provide warmth and light. People who arrive late because of physical difficulties are greeted warmly, rather than being treated as interruptions. New members who need to vent their fears are allowed to do so, as everyone listens patiently. In fact, there is no time pressure for the meetings, which just seem to flow comfortably.*

  Because Ruth is such an approachable person, she seemingly knows everyone, and the group is visited each week by another high-powered speaker in the area of heart health whom she has managed to persuade to give time voluntarily for this group.

  One of the group members remarked, "She makes everyone she interacts with feel important."

Would a dominant, decisive and somewhat impatient person have the same success in leading this group? Or someone whose impulse is to seek center stage? I doubt it.

And some groups need a perfectionistic, careful fact-checker, like Roger, who supervises workers in the manufacture of medical devices. He is proud of the fact that he contributes to making lives better, even in some cases, saving them, and he not only monitors the behavior of himself and the people he supervises to make sure it's up to standard, but he validates the importance of their work to each and every employee. He says, "Most of my life, people laughingly told me I was too 'picky.' By contrast, my first manager in this field always reminded me of how proud I could be of my careful work because it was so essential to the quality of life for many people. I just try to pass this along to the people I work with."

Why Study Different Normal Styles of Behavior, Perception and Learning?

You can:

- Have an explanation for other people's behavior that is not too self-referent.
  (They're not doing it *to me*, that's just what they do.)

- Adjust your behavior to ease a situation, recognizing and avoiding pushing other people's "hot buttons," and recognizing your own "hot buttons" for what they are.

("I'm getting tense because that other person is speaking so strongly, but I understand that it's just her style, and is not directly threatening me.")

- Speak the right "language" in order to be understood.

  - *Carol, an S, was concerned about her weight, and would often say to her mother, a high D, "I feel so fat," or "I look chunky in this outfit." Her mother would reply, "Nonsense, dear, you look just fine."*

    Carol, frustrated, felt her mother didn't understand her, until she understood that her indirect communication was going over the head of her mother, a high D direct communicator.

    She practiced, went to her mother, took a deep breath, and said, "Mother, I am concerned about my weight and it is affecting my self-esteem. I would like to see a doctor for a good weight-loss program and I need your support." Her surprised mother said, "Of course."

Reframe your descriptions of your own behavior and the behavior of other people to get a very different perspective. People can go "off the scale" in their behavior, and overuse their strengths to the point of weakness. The trick is to determine if that is what is happening in the situation you are observing, or whether it is simply that you have one standard for human behavior and the other person is someone "violating" that standard.

When you are describing the behavior of someone else that makes you uncomfortable, are you really describing what the person is doing, or are you describing your discomfort and lack of understanding of what the person is doing?

- *When the family of Leslie, an S, moved to another country, she was uncomfortable in the local school, and told her mother the other girls "didn't like her." Her D mother pooh-poohed her fears, and told her she was being "overly sensitive." Later, her mother discovered that in fact, people in this country were very aloof from newcomers, and needed time to overcome their suspicions. She learned that her daughter often could recognize subtle behaviors that she herself overlooked. A better label for her daughter might be "intuitive." With that understanding, her mother could listen carefully and help her daughter manage this quality so that it became a useful tool rather than a pathway to being overly suspicious and reclusive.*

Here are some reframing challenges:

If you have a Dominant person in your environment whose behavior seems somewhat threatening or unpleasant to you, ask yourself, is this behavior "decisive" and "quick," or is it closer to "bullying"? What are some differences you can observe to make this determination?

Sometimes people label the charming and energizing behavior of the I as "phony." When might that be true, and when might the I be simply trying to do what they do best, lifting other people's spirits?

An S who enjoys going along with the crowd may be labeled a conformist, yet the S may very well be getting greater pleasure from being part of the group than by taking an individual path. What might be the difference between being a conformist and being a harmonious team member?

Sometimes a C may be a "nitpicker," and sometimes the C may be slowing down to do some very important fact-checking. How can you tell the difference?

All of these challenges occur frequently in daily life, and there are no easy answers. However, it can be rewarding to note the great variety of human behavior and the motivation behind it – a little like a giant puzzle with which we are confronted every day. Engaging with the puzzle can definitely take you out of focusing on your own self-conscious discomfort as you become intrigued with the overall game of life.

Action steps for Chapter 4:

1. What is your idea of a "normal" person? Where did these ideas come from? How closely do you fit this picture of "normal"?

2. List your strengths. Ask a good friend to do the same for you.

3. List what you think might be your drawbacks. Can you reframe them as strengths? Can you think of situations

in which your qualities can function as strengths? When might they be less than effective?

Chapter 5:
Handling Criticism Effectively

Ask a group of people if anyone in the room *loves* criticism, and you'll find one or two people who actually raise their hands! Most, however, wince at the thought.

In Chapter 1, we learned about Bea, the would-be artist who never received credit for her artistic ability because she didn't dare exhibit her work for others to see. Why? She might receive criticism, and she couldn't *stand* it!

Philip Zimbardo found that cultures that use shame and blame when children make mistakes had much higher levels of shyness than cultures where trying and making a mistake was considered better than not trying.

Criticism can be shattering to self-esteem. At the same time, we wince at the thought of no standards: what if anyone was allowed to do brain surgery, or drive heavy equipment, or...the list is endless.

Critics of the subject of self-esteem sneer that it is a movement that focuses on making people feel good at the expense of quality. The implication is that proponents of self-esteem believe that correcting someone's efforts will result in lowered self-esteem; therefore, such correction is to be avoided. The critics maintain if you are never corrected in your efforts to learn a skill, your skill level will probably not be very high.

So how do we reconcile the need for standards with the need for human beings to feel whole and respected? First, we need to distinguish between "criticism" and "feedback." And we also need to recognize that criticism, or feedback, can come from others or from within. To which do you pay attention?

Feedback vs. Criticism

Some definitions of criticism include: censure, disapproval, disparagement, condemnation, and denigration. "Praise" is listed as an antonym, or a word that means the opposite of criticism.

But another set of definitions of the word "criticism" includes: analysis, appreciation, assessment, evaluation, review – neutral and even positive words. Do these definitions come immediately to your mind when you hear the word *criticism*?

In order to avoid any misunderstanding, let's use the word *feedback*: comments intended to provide useful information for future decisions and development.

What are some of the differences between the usual use of the words *criticism* and *feedback*?

Backwards or forwards?

Criticism tends to look backwards at what went wrong; *feedback* looks both forward and back, to provide information about how to improve performance in the future.

The assumption is that there will always be another chance.

Take responsibility for mistakes

When I called a company to complain about the quality of the product they had sent me, and the representative I complained to said warmly, "I'm glad you told me that! It should never have happened," my anger disappeared, and we worked together to solve the problem quickly.

How different it would have been if she had gotten defensive and denied the problem. We both would have been stressed, and the problem would have continued.

Defending yourself when you actually have made a mistake sets up a situation from which even a socially-adept person finds it difficult to exit.

And mistakes don't count nearly as much as you might think. Small social mistakes may, in fact, make you even more approachable and likeable. Do you really want to know someone who never makes a mistake and is always perfect?

Blame sounds final, and as if the person who committed the error is flawed in some way.

Responsibility suggests the presence of someone who is working towards a goal.

Setback vs. failure

When you make a mistake, even when you have not met a desired goal, you are not necessarily a failure. You have had a setback.

Failure sounds permanent; *setback* suggests a temporary block on the way to a goal.

Secure people may gulp after a setback, give themselves 24 hours to feel emotional, and then set to work analyzing why this setback occurred. Insecure people are devastated by failure.

Feedback can be both positive and negative

To be told only that you are wrong fails to tell you what *to do*. It can even bring you to a halt, with no map of how to proceed.

- *Matt, a dance teacher, often proclaimed loudly to his students and their parents, "I don't have to tell you when you're right. You know when you're right. My job is to tell you when you're wrong."*

But often we don't know when we're right. The little child who says to a relative, "You look just like a horse," is trying to unravel social rules about truth and lying. (The author actually did this – at a very young age.) The dancer or athlete trying to master a complicated movement that involves both very large and very fine muscle groups doesn't automatically know what to do, and needs to be guided by both positive and negative comments: "Yes, that's right," "No, that's wrong."

Tone of voice: neutral vs. emotional

Another difference is in tone of voice: "I *told* you not to go that way" (stressing the word "told" so that it sounds critical). Sometimes the tone of voice alone can determine the difference between criticism and feedback. And the word(s) emphasized can make a difference for both listener *and* critic.

Criticism	**Feedback**
Looks backwards	Looks to the future
Blames	Emphasizes responsibility
Provides anxiety	Provides information
Accusatory tone of voice	Neutral tone of voice
Perceives a Failure	Perceives a Setback
Negative	Positive and/or negative

So how can you get more feedback and less criticism from the world?

- Learn to give yourself feedback instead of criticism. Watch what you say to yourself when you make a mistake. Do you call yourself names? *Mary typically says, "Oh, stupid, stupid Mary," to herself when she makes a mistake.*

  Instead, look for what you can change about how you did something (your performance) in the future. Suppose you feel you really botched a job interview. Instead of blaming yourself, as Mary (above) did, say something such as, *"Next time I'll do a little more research on a company before I apply for a job,"* or *"Perhaps I could get a friend to role-play job interviews with me."*

  You may not always be aware of what you are saying, but if you feel bad, you are probably engaging in self-blame. Stop and take a deep breath. Try to figure out what the message actually is that you are giving yourself.

- Practice giving feedback instead of criticism to others. Sometimes you will have to take a deep breath to get into "neutral" and to use a calm tone of voice to give feedback:

  - *Rich picked up a bag of wet garbage in the kitchen to take to the garage. It burst, littering the kitchen floor with garbage.*
    Criticism: *"That was a stupid thing to do."*
    Feedback: *"I have found that when you carry the*

whole garbage pail out to the garage and lift the sack directly into the garbage can, you can avoid that kind of accident."

- Ask for feedback from people who are giving you only criticism.
  Annie had an office manager who frequently gave her criticism, which hurt her, and furthermore she didn't understand why or what he meant. He would often say, "You're so aggressive," when she thought she was simply being direct. Concerned about her upcoming job review, she asked for feedback: "What did I say when you felt I was being aggressive?" and "What would you have said in that situation?" She was asking for exact information about what she could do better in the future.

  He had been telling her only what *not* to do. He had been giving her a personality assessment, as he saw it. Furthermore, he hadn't really described her behavior, since *aggressive* is a word that can be interpreted many ways.

- Choose your critics!
  Select someone who genuinely has background in the area where you want advice. How do you know this person is an expert? In some fields, it is easy to determine if someone has credentials or expertise, such as a pharmacist. But what about someone who gives advice on an area where there are no specific training or credentials, such as human relations? Ask yourself if the person demonstrates capability in that area.

Sometimes you must educate a critic, as Annie had to do with her manager. Insist that they be clear. Ask them to help you improve, and ask them what you should do to improve. If they cannot, you might suspect that the critic has another agenda that has little to do with helping you improve your performance.

Praise

So far we have focused on the negative side of feedback. Let's look at the other, positive side: praise.

One of the interesting things about criticism is that people tend to think it is somehow more "real" than praise. Or, even if the praise is seen as "real," people can think that the one giving the praise has an ulterior motive, and therefore the praise should be refused.

- Reciprocity is not necessary.
  Receiving a compliment does not automatically require that you also give one back – it is not an obligation and does not have to be reciprocal. Just because you suspect that someone is complimenting you in order to get something from you, doesn't mean the compliment isn't real. Accepting it with a "thank you" does not mean you are obligated to return the favor or do anything else you don't wish to do.

- "The praiser has lousy standards."
  When you reject praise rather than accepting it with a

gracious, "thank you," you are being critical of the person offering the praise. You are suggesting the person may have low standards, or worse yet, be dishonest.

Who would dare to praise you again after such an experience?

- Unconditional love exists – if you can recognize it. Everyone seems to be looking for unconditional love; however, few people recognize it when it is given.

  - *Christine, a dancer, was complaining loudly in the dressing room that her mother always came to her performances and said, "You were the best one there." "How could she possibly know that?" asked Christine. "She doesn't know anything about dancing."*

Christine failed to recognize several things. The first is this: friends and loved ones want to be supportive, and what they may really be saying is something like, "I love you no matter what happens." In fact, it is a statement of unconditional love.

It is possible to say a sincere "thank you" to such praise without believing that it is objectively true. To fail to say "thank you" to someone who praises you, or worse yet, to sneer, "How would *you* know," is insulting to the speaker. It also teaches the person not to try to say anything like that in the future.

If you want an honest and useful opinion of your ability in a given field, go ask an expert!

People with low self-esteem often seem to solicit opinions from everyone around them: "How do I look?" "Do you really think I did well?" or compare themselves with the wrong people.

- *Terrilyn was in an entrepreneurship program, setting up a small business. She was feeling the agony of self-blame and doubt because she saw other people in the program advancing far faster than she did. Someone had to point out to her that the others who were doing so well had a far stronger and longer business background than she did. It's a little like faulting yourself for not doing better in a race when everyone else started yards ahead of you.*

Or they may go back to the same person over and over for the same lack of validation, or set up tests for themselves that almost seem meant to be failed.

To be able to evaluate criticism and critics, ask for feedback, deal courteously with others who make mistakes, and take responsibility for your mistakes; these are all the marks of someone with good self esteem – someone others want to be around.

- Construct a positive world for yourself.
  If you have a tape running in your head all of the time in which you are critical of your own behavior or that of others, you have created a critical world in which you are forced to live.

Try the exercises at the end of this chapter to help reconstruct your world into a more positive and pleasant place.

- Give up too much perfectionism.
  Perfectionism – the insistence that there be no mistakes in even the smallest detail – is fine in small doses. As an overall life plan, it is exhausting and doomed to failure.

Some areas where perfectionism is a good idea:

Anything involving safety of both property and human life, including:
    Operating heavy equipment
    Medicine, for example surgery, or mixing and administering medication
    Teaching and evaluating other people who will be involved in safety issues

Any field in which there is a strong need for precision in numbers and measurement, including:
    Finance
    Research
    Manufacture of precision tools and instruments

Areas where perfectionism is a very bad idea include:
    Human relationships
    Child rearing
    Home care
    Personal appearance

People with low self-esteem often agonize over small mistakes that other people don't notice or remember. In fact, someone who seems to be too perfect is often feared and disliked. An occasional mistake on your part can make your observer feel relieved that you, too, are human.

- Become a people magnet.
  Become someone who can give feedback instead of criticism to others. Provide helpful information in a way that helps another person move forward. Learn to feel comfortable giving and receiving praise. People will flock to know you!

And learn to deal fairly with yourself. You are never going to be fault-free. Neither is anyone else.

Randy Pausch, the terminally ill teacher whose "The Last Lecture" can be seen on YouTube, said, "The No. 1 goal as a teacher is to help students learn how to judge themselves."

Action steps for Chapter 5:

1. When you make a mistake, or assume you have made a mistake, try to calm down and give yourself feedback rather than self-criticism about it.

2. Notice others around you: do they give criticism or feedback to others?

3. List the situations in your life where perfectionism is important. Write down times when perfectionism has helped you reach an important goal. Then make another list of times when perfectionism has had a negative effect on your life.

4. Think back to the last time you made an embarrassing mistake. Did that one mistake really have negative consequences in your life? Or was it simply a case where you continued to feel embarrassed, and even started to avoid other peoplc or similar tasks and events?

Chapter 6:
What Do I Say When …?

Introverts prefer in-depth conversations to small talk, and shy people can be terrified of both. The motivation to avoid conversational situations is very powerful, but if you have a vision of the relationship you would like to have, how do you plan to find that relationship if you stubbornly refuse to interact with others? The fact is, in order to find that ideal Prince or Princess, you are at least going to have to shake hands with a lot of Frogs.

Learning the skills that smooth the way to interaction is a great way to reduce anxiety, and as you practice those skills, you may find you look forward to more and more interaction. This will not change you from an introvert to an extrovert, but it will go a long way towards making you a confident introvert.

Even if you choose to avoid many social settings, you will inevitably be a part of some of them, and you will be faced with awkward questions and comments that you can, with a little effort, learn to handle skillfully.

Remember: you will always have a choice as to whether to attend an event, speak with others or not. Wouldn't you like it to be a choice, and not something you're forced to avoid because you don't know what to do or say?

Establishing your Identity

Over and over, I hear shy people complaining that people don't understand them, and they're right. People don't. Why? Because shy people – and non-shy introverts, too – fail to provide enough information for other people to get a clear picture of whom they are dealing with.

So what do people do? Make things up. We all do it; we hear a few snippets of information about someone, and assume we know a lot about that person's level of intelligence, preferences, value system, amount of creativity, and more, when in fact we know less than we would know about an iceberg when we observe its tip standing out of the water. That's what stereotypes are all about: one label leads to a host of conclusions.

If you want people to know who you are, you will have to provide a few tidbits of information every now and then that will help them to establish the identity you want them to know.

Any one of us can find ourselves in a situation that is difficult or awkward to handle, and it can take skill to get out of the situation. But through their insecurity, people who lack self-confidence almost seem to *create* such difficult situations. Remember the story about Darrell in Chapter 3?

• *Darrell was a little nervous on the first day of his new job, so when another employee, who had worked there longer, addressed him as "Donald," he didn't correct him. He was too insecure on the second, third, and following days to make the correction. A year and a half later, he had still not told his co-worker his correct name, and the co-worker was still calling him Donald. Even a very confident person might feel a little foolish to make the change at that point, but a very confident person wouldn't have gotten into this dilemma in the first place.*

Darrell was too unsure of himself even to make sure others knew his real name, much less any other information that would have defined him as an individual.

Insecure people are in constant danger of being misunderstood because they lack the conversational skill to present a clear, strong picture of their identity.

To build communication skills, let's start with an important topic that all shy people face, no matter how much they may try to avoid contributing to a conversation.

Dealing With Awkward Questions

Most shy people have had the experience of feeling like a captive, immobilized because of another person's forward question asked, sometimes publicly, such as: "Why don't you have any children?" "Are you seeing anyone?" "Do you dye your hair?" or the most frequently heard, "Why are you so quiet?" Often, shy people blurt out the answer to a personal question, feeling they have no other choice, but then they become angry at themselves.

Let's look at some more comfortable ways to deal with these questions.

- Buy time to think
  First, you could practice some time-buying statements,
  such as:
  "Why are you asking"? (said with mild curiosity)
  "That's an interesting question. I'm sure it has
  different answers for different people."

  If you feel the question is really rude, you might say,
  "Would you repeat the question, please?" (If the
  questioner knows that it was rude, but did it anyway,
  he or she may feel uncomfortable about repeating it.)

  If you can't think of what to say immediately, just
  repeat the question thoughtfully: "Why did I quit
  medical school to go into publishing?"

- Buy time to make a decision
  If you feel uncomfortable because you're being rushed
  into making a decision:
  "I don't have an answer for you right now. I need some
  time to think."
  "This is too important to decide quickly. Let me think
  about it."
  "I'm not willing to make that decision right now."
  "I'm not sure how I feel about what you're asking. Let's
  discuss this a little later."

- Explore their motivation
  - *When Donna was first divorced, she learned to
    dread the question, "Are you seeing anyone?" She
    was ashamed and resentful when she had to
    answer, "No." The first question was often*

100

followed by, "You mean you went to that party/show/vacation spot alone?" And with great unease, she would often answer, "Yes."

Donna assumed that the questions and the answers she felt forced to give reinforced what she already suspected was true about herself: that she was a very unlovable human being – and here was simply more proof.

Many people, single or divorced, have told me of a similar uncomfortable reaction. Donna's solution at the time was to avoid those who asked these questions, because they were too painful for her to deal with. Even though she had resolved to solve her personal problems before becoming involved in another long-term relationship, she felt isolated in her loneliness.

Some years later, she again met an old friend who had often asked her about going places alone. This time, she answered more firmly and with a little pride, "Yes, I never let anything stop me from doing what I want to do." Her friend's response? "You're so brave! I could never do that!" And Donna began to see that often the motivation for these questions was not that of criticism, but of curiosity: "How is it possible for you to do this? Where do you get the strength?" And perhaps a little envy, also.

If she had paused before reacting emotionally, and instead had questioned the person asking, she might have spared herself a great deal of discomfort. But she initially reacted to her *assumptions* about what the friend was communicating, not the simple question itself.

- Question the question(er)
  That frequent, annoying question, "Why are you so quiet?" can strike terror into the heart of a shy person.

  You might want to use questioning to try to determine the motivation behind the question: Was it really said just to embarrass you or is the person unaware that this is an embarrassing question?
  "Is it important to you?" (to know why I don't have children, am unemployed right now, never got into major league baseball, have a scar on my face, etc.)
  "What is the basis for your question?"
  "Are you feeling critical of my actions?"
  "Is this something you would not do? Why?"

  The key to keeping your dignity in this kind of conversation is to use a very mild, non-accusatory, non-defensive tone of voice. Instead, look and act curious, because the other person may be motivated by something so far from your own interpretation that you may be startled. And in doing so, you will have enlarged your view of the world.

- Make an observation
  "Isn't it interesting how uneasy we can become when we meet people different from ourselves?"

- Deflect

  Finally, just because someone asks you a personal question doesn't mean you have to give them the answer they want. They may have control of the question, but *you* have control of the answer.

  Suppose you are currently working at a low-level, boring job, and someone at a party asks, "What do you do?" And let us suppose that you feel deflated every time you say, "I wash dishes in a hotel." You could say, "I work in a hotel during the day, but my real passion is photography," or," I work at this job because it leaves me free to participate in little theater productions." Then you can go on and describe enthusiastically what you are doing – or your questioner may even start asking questions about that subject.

  Unless you are actually in a formal or informal job interview situation, the motivation of the questioner is often to find out more about you and what you like to do in order to find mutual interests. So provide the other person with that kind of information, not your job resume.

What do you *do*?

One question we get asked frequently in the United States is, "What do you *do*?" This is considered to be a rude question in many other places in the world. Why do we ask it so much in the United States? We are heavily invested in our work, and identify with it. And we have set up a supposedly "classless" society, in which we have the image of the "self-made man (or woman)." In many other countries, your status is assigned to you at birth, and it can be difficult to change. In the United States, we *assume* anybody can be anything, and if you are not anyone very important right now, the question becomes "Why not?"

- *Rick attended a party given by a faculty couple at a prestigious university. The guests were almost all Ph.D.'s, distinguished authors, researchers, even a Nobel Prize winner.*

  During the evening, someone asked him, "And what do you do?" He burst out angrily, "Why do we always need to know what someone does? Why is this interesting?"

  Rick was a friend of the hostess, who had met him when she did some part-time work at a local organization. They had become friends on the basis of a similar sense of humor and similar political convictions. He was the only one there without a college degree, and he clearly found it painful. The questioner was undoubtedly trying to find a topic of mutual interest but Rick felt it as a potential criticism of his status.

Your answers should reflect enthusiasm and choice. When you answer a question you don't want to answer, you can feel like a victim.

Perhaps someone questions you at a time in your life when you feel you haven't achieved as much as you would like. Perhaps your money ran out when you were pursuing a college degree or owning a business. Physical problems may have stopped you from continuing in athletics. Layoffs and reorganization could have affected your career path.

Or perhaps you vastly prefer a simpler life, uncomplicated by too much straining for rewards, status, and material goods.

In these situations, you need a ready answer that sustains your own self-esteem. The answer should include both *enthusiasm* and *choice*.

The enthusiasm can be expressed in the warmth and forcefulness of your voice.

What about "choice"? Did you really choose to be laid off? No, but the next day after it happened, you began to make choices to move forward when you drew up your resume and notified your friends that you were in the job market, and registered for a class to increase your skills.

Once again, it is important to be able to describe what you do and what your interests are, because if you don't, other people will make up a life story for you.

Remember the "introvert" as described in Chapter 1? Another awkward moment occurs for shy introverts when they are asked, "What did you do over the weekend?" or, "What did you do for the holidays?" A shy introvert fears being judged as "not normal" for wanting some time alone. Learn to say, with enthusiasm, something such as, "I *really* had a chance to relax!" or, "I caught up with a lot of ... (letters, gardening, organization, hobbies)."

You can then deflect by commenting on some recent news item or an interesting book you have read – or by asking about the other person's weekend or holiday. (Often people ask about your weekend or holiday when they really want to tell you about theirs!)

Once again, project enthusiasm and choice in your response.

Conversation

One of the ways in which people assume someone is shy is if the person doesn't talk very much. As we have seen, this can happen for a number of good and bad reasons, but one of them is undoubtedly social anxiety. And sometimes that anxiety arises because the person hasn't learned the skill of conversation.

This is a pity, because the deep conversations that shy people and introverts favor don't happen by accident. Someone has to start connecting with someone else; an exchange of information has to take place before both parties can recognize that they have something in common.

How to be a great conversationalist: Listen

This is what introverts do best. So why not start to get a reputation as a great conversationalist by learning to listen?

Shy people frequently get so caught up in their own anxiety and discomfort ("What should I say next?" "They probably think I'm dumb.") that they are not really listening.

Few people really know how to listen to others, and when it happens, the person who feels listened to is surprised and grateful. And you don't have to talk much; you just need to encourage the speaker to give more information.

Encouraging body language

Looking at the speaker, nodding affirmatively every now and then, saying, "uh huh" in an approving tone, all encourage someone else to continue speaking.

Ask questions to encourage the speaker to continue

Suppose a friend mentions having vacationed in Hawaii. You ask, "Did you like it?" You have asked a closed-end question, one that can only be answered by a "yes" or a "no."

If the friend isn't a great conversationalist, the conversation will die after that one-word answer.

You might try again: "How was the weather?" If it rained every day, you friend might make a face and give a very short answer.

But what if you ask, "What are some of the things you liked about your trip?" Notice the phrase "some of the things" because it will probably elicit several comments you never imagined. This is an example of an open-ended question, which can unlock a floodgate of conversation because it allows the speaker to make choices about what to say.

Brief open-ended questions that can draw other people out include:
When did you realize you wanted to be an engineer?
How long have you been so interested in photography?
Where have you traveled during your career?
What are some of the things you like best about your job?
"Tell me about it!" This is my favorite that you can use when someone mentions having had any kind of experience, from a visit to the theater to a job change to travel.

This last phrase gives the speaker license to select anything he or she *wants* to talk about.

Having a Dialogue

Many people don't speak up much because they are afraid of sounding foolish. Others are so painfully self-conscious they can't think of anything to say after they've said "hello." Then there are those who can talk, but it isn't conversation.

- *Andrew tried to make himself an expert on any topic he encountered. There is nothing wrong with doing this; it was how he used the information that marked him as insecure. When he was in a group, he would say, "Say, did you know about ...?" and instruct the group. He especially did this if someone brought up a topic on which he was not an expert; he just changed the subject to one on which he was an expert. He was not very popular because he didn't grasp that conversation is a two-way street, not an occasion to display what you know and to be admired.*

Not everyone is born with the "gift of gab," or has good models. Sometimes communication and conversation are skills that have to be learned.

Conversation is a little like a tennis match; each person has to lob the ball back to the other person for a true dialogue to occur. And each person has to have some motivation to continue the conversation.

Keeping the Conversation Going

Give some free information

You don't have to brag or deliver a monologue to let someone know your interests and your skills.

Perhaps you are with one or more other people who are discussing a movie with an historical background. Suppose the movie is about the Civil War, and you say, "I visited Gettysburg once, and I was amazed at how close the two armies were when they were firing at each other."

Now the listener knows you have enough interest in history to travel to an historic site.

Suppose you are complimented on your cooking. You remember visiting your grandmother, who taught you a lot of skills, so you say: "Thanks, I used to help my grandmother in her restaurant when we would visit her in Iowa."

You've just filled in the picture of yourself with four pieces of "free information": You had a grandmother you have fond memories of, you used to enjoy helping her, you have some restaurant experience, and you have visited Iowa.

Build "hooks" into your conversation

Furthermore, you have built "hooks" into your conversation. Hooks are things you have said that another person can pick up on and comment or ask questions, such as: "Oh, what part of Iowa?" or "How old were you when you worked in her restaurant?"

And be sure you listen for and pick up on "hooks" in other people's conversations.

It's Not Just What You Say, It's How You Say It

Voice

If you have difficulty speaking in public, don't just think about what you would like to say – practice speaking, and do it out loud. You could choose to read a favorite poem, a paragraph from a book, or an article from your newspaper out loud.

It is even better if you can record your voice and listen to yourself speak.

These are some things to keep in mind as you speak:
- Before you start, try humming a familiar song to warm up your voice and to relax your vocal muscles.
- Imagine a person or group to whom you are speaking.
- Look at this imaginary person or group as you speak.
- Take several deep breaths before you start.
- Keep your voice *low* and *slow*.
- Think of what the words mean, and try to put that meaning into your voice.

Eye contact

Eye contact is an important part of communication, but it is also one of the most misunderstood.

Appropriate eye contact varies from culture to culture, and is loaded with meaning. In some cultures, it is disrespectful to look directly into the eyes of someone who is of higher status or authority. In other cultures, a woman is judged as being too open sexually if she looks directly at men.

In American business culture, there are a number of meanings attached to eye contact, or the lack of it. People who do not make confident eye contact may be judged as:
- Dishonest
- Lacking in confidence
- Lacking skill
- Not interested

It has been said that people do not "buy" skills; they "buy" confidence; that is, they evaluate other people based on the confidence that person exudes, not the level of skill they may have. Eye contact with others, including managers and bosses, which projects confidence, should be firm and direct, but not staring.

To make this kind of eye contact, imagine a circle on your listener's face, a circle which includes the tip of the nose at the lower end, the cheekbones at the sides. The top of the forehead completes the circle. While you are speaking and interacting with the listener, lightly scan this area. This will give the impression of alert attentiveness without staring fixedly into the other person's eyes, which can be very uncomfortable for both speaker and listener.

Communication Without Words

Displaying comfortable body language is important even when you are not in a conversation with others.

- *Consider the dilemma of Duane, who was concerned about where to look when he was walking in one direction and someone came toward him from the opposite direction. He confessed that he didn't know where to look. His heart would start pumping fast. He said, "At that moment, all I think about is how not to look nervous. What facial expression and body language should I project?"*

Duane revealed that he had even quit a job because of this problem.

This experience is very familiar to many shy people. Here are some tips for looking and feeling more comfortable.

- Take up some physical activity, if you have not already done so. If team sports make you uncomfortable, try something solo: swimming, rollerblading, ice skating, skiing, yoga, martial arts, dancing (by yourself, in your living room, if necessary). Find some instruction. You can even practice competitive sports such as tennis and golf by yourself with the help of a Wii system that works on your TV. The point is to loosen up and get used to moving your body in different ways.

- Walk as if you have a purpose. Feel the soles of your feet pressing firmly into the sidewalk, floor, or path.

- Breathe slowly and deeply.

- Look into the distance as if you are moving towards something desirable – a meeting with a friend, an important errand, something pleasant. Don't frown. If you think of something pleasant, such as a friend or an activity you enjoy, your face will have a comfortable expression.

- Better yet, become "mindful" of your environment. To be mindful is to pay close, interested attention to details around you: trees, foliage, signs, buildings, cars – and even people.

And above all, remember this: those people passing you are caught up in their own inner thoughts, hopes, and fears. They're not looking at you, and they are not judging you. They may even be having the same fears you are having! In fact, if the figures we have about shyness in the U.S. population are accurate, they probably are at least as uneasy as you are!

If all of the above tips on conversation sound complicated and exhausting, just remember to focus on being interested in other people in all their differences, ideas, and experiences.

Action steps for Chapter 6:

1. Listen to a conversation between two people, perhaps at a party, in an office, or on public transportation. Can you recognize the "hooks" that people may put into their conversations onto which the listener can grab and continue that conversation? Can you recognize when someone fails to grab a hook that was offered?

2. One reason shy people dread large group settings is the fact that they may have to project their voices over a distance and over other conversation in order to be heard. If you are going to have to project your voice over any distance (as in a workplace meeting or a class), you may be concerned that you will be too faint, or worse yet (from the point of view of a shy person), that you will find your voice blaring out over everyone else's.

Here's how to practice "throwing" your voice over a distance. Once again, it is even better if you can record yourself speaking. Think of the recorder (or another "target," if you don't have a recorder) as a basket such as you would find in basketball.

Stand six feet away from the target, and say, "My name is ...." Try to imagine that your voice is the ball, and you are trying to drop it in the basket. If you have a recorder, add, "... and I am standing six feet away from the basket." This will help you because the exercise is to repeat the statement at different distances from the "target." Vary the distance, so that you get used to projecting your voice over different distances.

3. Introverts and shy people often maintain that they prefer deep conversation to idle chitchat. Think about what you mean by the phrase "deep conversation." What might the topic be? How could you introduce it to test the waters and see if the other person is interested in having a conversation on this topic?

Chapter 7:

The Great Adventure: Risking the Change

For of all sad words of tongue or pen,
The saddest are these: "It might have been!"
John Greenleaf Whittier

We come now to the topic that should really be the start of
your quest for a more confident life: risk-taking. But I have
left it until now so that you could learn the various skills that
you will call upon when you start.

Before you shudder and back away, recognize that you have
been taking risks all of your life. For it is a risk to remain
hidden, to conceal your talents, to withhold your opinion. By
doing so, you risk having your life's course determined
entirely by other people and by outside events.

---

*And the day came when the risk to remain tight in a
bud was more painful than the risk it took to blossom.*
~Anais Nin

If you feel that change is too risky, think about the risk of
staying in one place and refusing to change. Change <u>will</u> come
to you: jobs will end, careers will shift, health will swing back

and forth between robust and less-than-optimal, relationships will alter and even disappear.

If changes come to you unexpectedly, you are forced to cope with them when you are overwhelmed by surprise and the accompanying emotions. Why not learn risk-taking skills when you are in charge of the risk because you are making a choice as to *what* to risk? It is much less dangerous.

The greatest risk of all is this: when people are dying, they don't regret what they have done; they very much regret what they might have done, but didn't.

To practice risk-taking is to hone a very important skill, one that will help you to feel more secure for the rest of your life. And risk-taking *is* a skill, one that can be learned and practiced.

"Brave" and "fearless" are not the same thing.

Successful people take risks, and the stories of the risks they take can fill volumes. Did they feel fear? Of course they did. To be brave is not to be fearless; it is to go ahead and do what you need to do in order to get to where you want to go even though you are afraid.

You will make mistakes. Everyone does. The trick is to become resilient, and the trick behind that is to learn a process that minimizes the danger of risk-taking. As George Patton, famous American general in WWII said, "Take calculated risks. That is quite different from being rash." Or to put it another way, don't jump off cliffs without being pretty sure there is a trampoline at the bottom!

By now, you have learned a number of techniques for navigating through the scary world of social connections, because that is how we defined shyness at the onset: anxiety that is active in social situations. Whether these social connections involve personal relationships or career associations is irrelevant. In both cases, people skills are of paramount importance.

To Change or Not To Change

Perhaps you have realized that you are an introvert: someone with a rich internal life who desires a small circle of close friends and who desires a certain amount of solitude. Your challenge may be to find, out of the bustling world, those few people with whom you want to have a deep connection.

Or you have discovered you are someone who desires a rich social life filled with many friends, or you have aspirations that will require you to find more social support in order to fulfill those aspirations.

Be very clear on your goal: what do you expect as a result of the changes you are willing to make?

Whatever your reasons, implementing your new skills will mean risking a change from your established pattern of behavior, and that always feels a little dangerous.

Beyond changing the ways in which you evaluate and communicate, let's look at some other kinds of risks you might need to take:

- Telling other people who you really are: your values and principles
- Revealing your dreams in order to find others to help you
- Striving for something you've always wanted

The Rewards of Risk-Taking

Before starting, why not list some of the benefits you will experience as a result of learning to take risks. Here are a few:

- Become more and more courageous and proud
- Open up your perception of what is available
- Make the world less dangerous for yourself

Setting up the "Trampoline" at the Bottom of the Cliff

Set a goal

What is the goal of your risk-taking plan? To feel comfortable in social situations? Too general. To meet someone with whom you can have a relationship? Too high and broadly-defined a goal for a first attempt.

These are great ultimate goals, but first you need a set of sub-goals. It's a little like the advice on eating an elephant: one bite at a time.

We've already looked at some small sub-goals in the earlier chapters. An example of a sub-goal might be to make eye contact and warmly greet one person today that you have seen in your building elevator, or say something good-humored and complimentary to a server in a restaurant. You could do this once a day for a week before escalating to your next sub-goal. (Check Chapter 6 to refresh your memory.)

Your next sub-goal might be to show some interest in another person – a classmate, co-worker, or neighbor, for example – by asking a question that helps the other person to reveal some information about his or her goals or interests. (Chapter 6 again.)

Why not risk going to a meeting or conference alone, and then asking people if you might join them at their table? Try your growing conversational skills.

If you feel uncomfortable after the event because you think your behavior was awkward, remember:

- You don't really know these folks, and you don't have to see them again.

- This is just practice for when you see someone you really want to know, or perceive an opportunity you would really like to take.

- If you dwell on how uncomfortable you felt, you will not want to try again. But that is what you must do, over and over, until it becomes easy.

Consider the reward in advance

You may want the outcome to be a new friend or relationship or a better job. These are fine outcomes, and you may need to pursue a number of sub-goals, all leading in the right direction, before you achieve these rewards.

But before you start, ask yourself the following question: "What is the *lowest* level reward I will accept and still feel that it was okay to go ahead and take the risk?" Some examples of lower level rewards are:

- Acceptance that your actions were a "practice run"
- Realization that you asked a question, such as, "Is this situation right for me?" and have taken steps towards achieving an answer
  Perhaps the answer is, "No, this isn't the right situation for me." You can then turn your time and energy in another direction.
- Recognition that you have gone beyond your "comfort zone" and survived

Set up a "Plan B" before you start

Plan B is something else you will do if your plan to master a goal doesn't exactly play out as you would like. It's not your favorite outcome, because if it were, it would be Plan A.

Why would you set up a Plan B? To overcome your tendency to think, "I'm going to dare to ... and *if I don't succeed, it will be awful!*"

Plan B allows you to think, "This isn't so bad. Well, I didn't succeed this time, but I took action, got some practice, and learned a lot about how to proceed when I try again. In the meantime, I can ... (fill in the blank with Plan B)."

An example of a Plan B success

Years ago, I took what seemed to be a gigantic risk – telling an important person in my life that I had developed personal feelings for him. I had no idea how he felt; but since I was losing sleep at night thinking about a possible relationship with him, I felt it was important to go ahead and take the risk because if I didn't do so, *I would never know whether it would have worked or not.* I would have been haunted for life.

For my Plan B, I set up a self-pampering session in advance of my going to see him. I would arrive home after the meeting and promptly call my favorite restaurant to have my favorite meal delivered. In the meantime, I would draw a scented bath, put on my favorite music, and take a bottle of my favorite wine out of the refrigerator. And I would congratulate myself for having had the courage to take the risk.

He refused the relationship; I carried out Plan B. And I found, as so many others have, that the result of having taken a well-planned risk, no matter what the outcome, is a sense of relief (I didn't have to obsess over that person any more), and even better, a sense of exhilaration at my courage. I congratulated myself, saying, "This was just practice for the next time I want to take such action. I'm getting better all the time!"

Remember that resorting to Plan B doesn't mean you're stuck with that choice for the rest of your life. It's just a way to deal with the temporary discomfort you will feel if you do not immediately achieve your highest goal.

Become both the Observer and the Actor

We typically become deeply immersed in emotional situations, making it difficult to think clearly and to remember all of the details afterwards. Yet it is important to be aware of what you do and say, in order to determine what you would like to do differently in the future.

Many fine performers and athletes learn the trick of being able to step back mentally and evaluate themselves in action. It is by this method that they improve their performance level without being overwhelmed by destructive emotions.

The trick is to split yourself into two "people," the Actor and the Observer.

- The Actor is your body going through the motions of taking the risk: what you say, how you say it, your body language.

- The Observer is your detached mental self whose only function is to perceive carefully what you do and say, in order to provide accurate feedback later.

Picture your Observer self mounted somewhere up in a corner of the room, looking down on your Actor self. The Observer is not critical because the Observer is not emotionally involved. The Observer provides feedback: information that you can use in the future to improve your actions. The Observer never compares you with other people!

A noted Olympian was once asked how he accomplished all the things he did. He replied, "I don't take myself seriously." His interviewer was shocked, but the athlete went on to say, "I take what I *do* very seriously." He had mastered this division into the Actor and the Observer.

Evaluate your performance fairly

Remember to use your skills in turning criticism, including self-criticism, into feedback. (Review Chapter 5, "Handling Criticism Effectively.")

Remind yourself that there are no failures, only setbacks. A setback can signal one of several things:

- You chose the wrong path to your goal and need to search for another path.
- You were under-prepared (for the exam, job interview, discussion of a conflict, etc.), but you will prepare better and try again. You just had a learning experience.

Setbacks provide information to you, if you let them. If you label them "failures" and become emotional, you will find you have reached a dead-end in your quest for a better life.

Know the difference between "stubbornness" and "persistence"

"If at first you don't succeed, try, try again," is a phrase most of us learned early in life. It can be dangerous if you don't truly understand what "trying again" involves.

"Persistence" is the ability to continue towards a goal, taking in new information and varying the paths by which you try to reach the goal. Persistence requires resiliency, the ability to come back after a setback and try again.

"Stubbornness" is the need to keep on trying the same thing over and over, in the hopes that this time the outcome will be better. To keep on trying again is like hitting your head against a stone wall; sooner or later, something will break, but don't count on it's being the stone wall.

And don't wait until you're pretty sure you won't make a mistake before you risk trying something new. That will never come; you will always make mistakes, and the world will not end.

One good way to practice your developing social skills is to join an existing organized group that already has a focus. Some examples are:

- A class – on photography, music, current events, spirituality, or whatever interests you
- A volunteer group – animal shelter, meals for the homeless

Initial rewards for joining a group include:
- Developing expertise in a subject so that you have something to talk about.
- Being in contact with other people in a way that does not focus specifically on relationships. Personal pressure is reduced when you all have a task to perform and to talk about.

Making Friends

Finding and making friends – people who support you and whom you can support – doesn't have to be threatening or hard. At first, you may need to have a plan, but soon you will find you are doing these things spontaneously.

"First Impressions" aren't indelible

Forget the phrase, "You only have one chance to make a first impression." It can keep you from ever making an attempt to reach out to others. People are so wrapped up in their own lives they are honestly not noting and recording everything you do. If you are an introvert, you may have blended so well into the wallpaper that you haven't even been noticed yet. If you have done something that you believe was spectacularly embarrassing, you may be stunned to find that no one remembers, particularly if you got over your discomfort and forgot about it yourself.

When I first started my program of confidence-building, I recognized that I had attended a major university without ever making a friend there. I decided to remedy that error by joining my alumnae club, which met every month. In the first year, I made every blunder a shy person can imagine: spilling water all over the table (and into everyone's laps), accidentally shooting my dessert across the table into the face of a Nobel Laureate, and more. At the end of the year, I was nevertheless asked to be Coordinator of Speakers for the group. Now, I don't think I was asked because I was felt to be the most outstanding candidate; it was a volunteer job, and there weren't too many volunteers available. But no one seemed to hold my examples of social awkwardness against me either. I held the job for five years, my confidence growing every year.

Meet

Meeting people is easy, particularly if you choose to meet them in structured situations. Conferences, classes, lectures and church socials are all examples of such situations. Be willing to introduce yourself to others, and to ask other people their names. Practice saying, *"Hi, my name is ..."* before you go out. Remember that people won't reject you or even remember you if the words come out with a stutter, or stick in your throat. Keep saying to yourself, "It's all practice!"

In public situations, practice saying something light to people you don't know, or hardly know. Try, *"Your wrists must get really tired by the end of the day"* to a supermarket clerk scanning canned goods, or, *"Serving the public can be rough, can't it?"* to a server that you have just seen being harassed by a rude customer. To someone sitting next to you in a theater or at a concert, you could remark, *"I'm excited to be here because I've been waiting for this for a long time."*

If you're an animal lover, or a dog walker, there is always a chance for conversation in parks and on walks. Even without a dog, you can admire others' pets, and ask questions about them.

Are you reluctant to talk to strangers? Remember, meeting is not connecting. You will probably not see these people again, or if you do, it will only be another brief encounter, so all you have done is gotten in some great practice.

If you are joining a group, listen to what members of the group have to say about what they believe is the purpose of the group.

- *Sara joined a book club, hoping to make friends. She was annoyed and felt rejected when some members of the book club held social events without her. The members of this book club were really serious about the books they were sharing, but based their friendships on a lot of other characteristics that Sara did not share, such as an interest in sports. She was mildly interested in the new books they were discussing, but not enough that she felt her needs had been met at the end of each meeting.*

If a group you consider joining is deeply focused on the activity that defines the group, you may not fit in unless you are equally dedicated. There's nothing wrong with you or them; you just don't fit together.

Connect

You can connect with people when you show some real interest in them as an individual. Remember in Chapter 6, when we talked about putting "hooks" into your conversations, and responding to other people's "hooks"?

- *Lisa went to a luncheon honoring an author and the launching of his new book. She was seated at a luncheon table with five other people who were students in the same academic department as the author.*

  Lisa had been practicing her social skills, so she went around the table asking names and introducing herself. She then turned to the person on her right, and asked about his activities. He became animated as he told her about his research. When he finished, she turned to the person on his right, and drew out the same information. In fact, Lisa went around the whole table quizzing the others, and giving them a chance to talk about the work that was most important to them. They all looked comfortable and animated during the recitals, but when the last one finished they all fell silent and began to look uncomfortable again.

Not one of them thought to ask Lisa about her activities!

It is very likely that the others didn't know what to do or say at this point.

If Lisa had been more socially skilled, she might have then proceeded to mention her interests, but she did not.

The paradox of shyness is that we sufferers feel insignificant and at the same time are so intensely focused on ourselves and our own discomfort that we sometimes act as if we are the center of the universe!

Connection must be a two-way street. Ask questions about other people's interests; offer some information of your own.

Share

This is where you offer some more in-depth information about yourself and gather deeper information about the other person. You might meet someone several times before deciding to share.

"What made you go into social work?" or "What prompted you to move to North Carolina?" are the kinds of questions that start to round out your picture of the other person.

Listen for the "hooks" and grab them by responding to them: "I read an article about how social workers need to fight job burnout," or "The travel section had an article recently on

North Carolina, with some beautiful pictures of ...."

Appreciate

Unless it is a work group where your effectiveness may be judged immediately by what you have to offer, or unless you are asked to do so, it is not good initially to offer plans that would change the structure and the focus of the group.

- *Amy joined a support group for cancer survivors. The group had been meeting for some time in a community center, which the leader often decorated with fresh flowers and candles for the meeting. Sharing of group members' experiences alternated with talks by experts on the latest research and treatments for cancer. The group members had become very comfortable with one another.*

  Amy (a shy extrovert) was eager to become a member of this group. In her first meeting, she announced that she would give a talk on alternative medications at one of the meetings, and that she would like to host a meeting at her home. The next time the group met, she arrived with written invitations for everyone to shift the following meeting to her home.

  The other members, who had become very comfortable with the way the group was developing, shied away from her. In no time at all, she was feeling shunned.

Think this is an unlikely scenario? When shy people decide to become bold and take a risk, they often do so before they have developed the skills to take an intelligent risk. Amy had only met these people; she hadn't connected with them. Yet she behaved as if she were the leader, when no one had indicated that she was.

Amy had made a mistake. Is this fatal? No, she became more subdued, but eventually joined in with the conversation, asking questions, responding to others, offering some of her own experiences, and expressing appreciation of ideas that other people contributed. Genuine appreciation of the contributions of others is a major key to connecting with them.

Recently, Astronaut Alan Bean revealed in an interview that he had taken up painting. The interviewer asked him if this was the result of a transcendental event that he experienced after having walked on the moon and looked back at the Earth from outer space. He said no, he had used the same skills that he had used to become an astronaut. *It's the same process. Study, practice, make mistakes.*

If I had not risked joining my alumnae group so long ago, consciously monitored my progress, learned to accept the discomfort of my mistakes, and continued, despite setbacks, I would not be enjoying the full, joyous life I am now leading.

And I certainly wouldn't be writing this book.

Action steps for Chapter 7:

1. Decide on a small risk you would like to take in the next week: going to a new environment, trying some new activity. Review all the steps a good risk-taker uses, and also go over the difference between feedback and criticism.

2. If you visit a new group or connect with a new person, and the connection somehow didn't work out, list all the reasons that might be so. Do NOT go into explanations that involve your deficiency in any way. Instead, list the reasons why it was not a good "fit" for you.

Chapter 8:

The Magic Bullet

There isn't one. Nope, no magic potion either. Magic rings are in short supply. The Yellow Brick Road holds some promise, but you must hold true to your vision, putting one foot in front of the other, repeatedly. This is the only way that people who are truly expert at living have found to create their most satisfying life.

Is it worth it? Review the pain you have felt that led you to read this book. Count the times you have felt slighted, underappreciated, overlooked, lonely. Then take a deep breath and commit to doing the work (yes, it is work) to change that. Only you can do so. Hundreds, thousands, and probably millions of people have done so. So can you.

A little secret here: it actually starts to be FUN as you go along.

Action steps for Chapter 8:

1. Use the following format to focus on and to track your progress as you step out and risk trying different behaviors:

My goal:

What action I took:

What worked:

What didn't work:

Why it didn't work (focus on Feedback, not Criticism):

My next step:

Chapter 9:

Living the Full Life

"The tragedy in the life of most of us is that we die before we are fully born."
~Erich Fromm

You must have had a vision of the life you desired when you started reading this book. Was it completely your vision, or did it have components that you thought you "should" have in your life, or that you felt were typical of a more "normal" person? Your style of happiness may be very different from anyone currently around you. Part of your quest for a better life is to get out and find those people whose vision is similar to yours, and who accept you gladly.

As you progress, you will find it easier and easier to say "No!" to thoughts that are not consistent with your growing self-image, and especially to say "No" to other people who want to provide direction to you that is not consistent with your true self.

Abraham Maslow, noted Humanistic Psychologist, describes what he believed to be the pinnacle of human development: Self Actualization. It is a glowing description of life as it could be, and it includes the following characteristics:
Acceptance of self and others
Spontaneity
Problem centering outside self rather than on oneself

Need for solitude, quiet reflection (Introverts are halfway there.)
Accepts imperfections – the self-actualizing person is comfortable with him- or herself, but never stops striving

Before reaching this pinnacle, however, the lower steps in the hierarchy must be dealt with. They include:

Biological needs:
The basic needs for life include air, water, and food. When these needs are not met, they become so urgent that paying attention to the higher needs, as described below, becomes difficult, if not impossible.

Safety and security:
Physical security involves shelter, stability, law and order. The need for physical security, like the biological needs, can distract you from reaching for anything higher.

Social insecurity is the very basis of low self-esteem. In this book we have developed the idea that high self-esteem is the ability to solve life's problems, and the recognition that you have that ability, even when the solution isn't immediately apparent.

Building confidence that you will find a solution that is not now present means that you must be patient, learn to relax and even distract yourself briefly from the immediate problem in order to allow your creative abilities to function. Any kind of stress, including the stress of feeling insecure, will block your ability to find a good solution. You must learn to have confidence in your ultimate problem-solving abilities. An excellent phrase to remember and to repeat to yourself is this: "There is a solution. I just can't see it right now."

Chapters dealing with problem-solving skills included Chapter 5 ("Handling Criticism Effectively"), Chapter 6 ("What do I say when ...?"), and Chapter 7 ("The Great Adventure: Risking the Change"). You have read them; did you complete the Action Steps? More than once?

Belongingness:
You can define how much belongingness you need to be truly healthy and happy. We do know that human beings need others. Introverts don't need to become the center of a large circle of friends; a few may be sufficient, but they are every bit as necessary to maintain well-being as a large circle is to an extrovert.

With well-developed social skills you can learn to identify and connect with those people who truly suit you. In the meantime, remember, you may have to brace yourself to approach and at least shake hands with a lot of Frogs before you find that Prince or Princess. How will you know, otherwise, who or what is out there?

As you circulate more, review Chapter 4 ("Discover How Others Misunderstand You") for tips on *why* you might feel uncomfortable or threatened around some people and relaxed with others.

Esteem:

When you learn to esteem yourself, you will be esteemed by others. Esteeming yourself will include letting other people know who you are and what are your skills and your preferences. It also includes esteeming others, and letting them know you do so. It is a two-way street, and you must be sure to walk both sides.

It is your responsibility to let other people know who you are; if you allow them to guess, they will either invent a story that you wouldn't recognize, or worse yet, won't even bother to get to know you. Review the section on conversations in Chapter 6 to refresh your memory on how to hold meaningful conversations with others.

Any skill takes a lot of practice, whether it is conversation, pole vaulting, or trumpet playing. No one masters it in one take. No one masters a skill without making mistakes. Once you recognize and accept these simple truths, you are ready to move forward.

You will sometimes feel you have made no progress, or even that you have slipped backward. As more than one wit has remarked, it's a little like cleaning your house – you just have to do it again in six months. Do you think you can do it – start a conversation, take a risk, say "no," reframe a negative as a positive, change criticism to feedback – just once, and there will be no more metaphorical dust bunnies or grease collecting? No, you'll have to do it again, and again. Each time you assert, calmly and with dignity, who you are and how you want to be treated, it gets to be a little easier and the problem a little less than it was originally.

Here are some of the rewards for being a confident introvert, or indeed, the rewards of being a confident human being:

An introvert can – and should be – proud of independence and the ability to do things on one's own, or just be alone without feeling that it is a form of punishment.

You don't need to try to match the temperament or preferences of those around you.

You now recognize – and are proud of – the many excellent qualities that an introvert can bring to different situations, including leadership positions.

You have the ability to ask for what you need, including time to think things over.

You can choose relationships; they don't just happen, or not happen, to you.

As a leader, you can structure group situations to include everyone, making you a stronger leader and making your group stronger.

And, if you practice the skills presented in this book, whether you are a shy extrovert or a less-than-confident introvert, you can connect with people who value you for who you are.

Whether you were motivated to read this book because you were an unconfident introvert, a shy extrovert, a parent puzzled by a child who seems very different from you, or a manager of people who wants to draw the very best from a team, I trust that you now have the ability to see yourself and others very differently, and some skills to start treating yourself and others very differently.

In *The Stress of Life*, Hans Selye, the "Father of Stress," wrote in an introduction the following words of wisdom. I would like to end this book with the same words.

"This book is dedicated to those who wish to enjoy the stress of a full life, and are not so naïve as to think they can do so without effort."

Like many authors, Lynette depends on the reviews and word-of-mouth referrals of her readers. Please consider leaving a review on Amazon.com, Barnesandnoble.com, or Goodreads.com.

Follow Lynette's blog at www.CreativeLifeChanges.com, and feel free to contact her at Lynette@CreativeLifeChanges.com about classes and coaching.

Recommended Reading

Cain, Susan: *Quiet: The Power of Introverts in a World That Can't Stop Talking*.
Motivated by personal experience, Susan Cain has delved deeply into research on introversion, the many ways in which it is positive, and the reasons why it has been marginalized for so long in our culture.
Crown Publishing, 2012.

Ellison, Sharon: *Taking the War Out of Our Words*.
Sharon Ellison is the creator of a system of non-defensive communication techniques through the use of carefully crafted questions. This is an in-depth how-to book on handling difficult communication situations.
Bay Tree Publishing, 2002.

Sources

Aron, Elaine. *The Highly Sensitive Person.*
Broadway Books, 1997.

Bandura, Albert. *"Self-efficacy: Toward a Unifying Theory of Behavioral Change."*
Psychological Review, 1977, Vol. 84, No. 2, 191-215.

Branden, Nathaniel. *The Psychology of Self-Esteem.*
Nash Publishing Corporation, 1969.

Cohen, Sheldon et al. *"Chronic Stress, Glucocorticoid Receptor Resistance, Inflammation, and Disease Risk."*
Proceedings of the National Academy of Sciences, 2012, 109 (16), 5995-5999.

Ericsson, K. Anders et al. *"The Role of Deliberate Practice in the Acquisition of Expert Performance."*
Psychological Review, 100, No. 3, 1993, 363-406.

Garfield, Charles. *Peak Performance.*
Warner Books, 1985.

Geier, John. *Personal Profile System.*
DiSC, 1977.*

Harris, Maxine, Ph.D. *The Loss That is Forever: The Lifelong Impact of the Early Death of a Mother or Father.* Plume, 1996

Henderson, Lynne, and Philip Zimbardo. *"An Overview of Shyness, What Is Known and How It Is Treated."* Encyclopedia of Mental Health, Academic Press, 1998, 497-510.

James, William. *Principles of Psychology.* Henry Holt & Company, 1890.

Kagan, Jerome, and Nancy Snidman. *The Long Shadow of Temperament.* Belknap Press of Harvard University Press, 2009.

Marston, William Moulton. *Emotions of Normal People.* Taylor & Francis Ltd., 1999; originally published 1928.

Maslow, Abraham. H. *"Hierarchy of Needs: A Theory of Human Motivation."* Psychological Review 50(4), 1943, 370-396.

Pulford, Briony, Andrew Colman, and Fergus Bolger. *"Businesspeople Who Are Too Sure Of Their Abilities Are Less Savvy Entrepreneurs."* Experimental Psychology, 55(2), 2008, 113-120.

Rengel, Peter. *Seeds of Light.* H J Kramer, 1987.

Schwartz, Carl E., et al. *"Inhibited and Uninhibited Infants 'Grown Up': Adult Amygdalar Response to Novelty."* Science, 20 June 2003, Vol. 300, no. 5627, 1952-1953.

Selye, Hans. *The Stress of Life.*
McGraw-Hill, 1956.

Zimbardo, Philip. *Shyness: What It Is, What To Do About It.*
Addison-Wesley, 1977.

Zimbardo, Philip, and Shirley Radl. *The Shy Child: A Parent's Guide to Preventing and Overcoming Shyness from Infancy to Adulthood.*
McGraw-Hill, 1981.

***

About the Author

Lynette Crane is an executive coach, corporate trainer, nationally acclaimed speaker, and author.

After spending her youth pursuing a career as a ballet dancer, she enrolled in college at the age of twenty-seven, transferring to Stanford University at the age of thirty. She felt extremely insecure about coming from a non-verbal profession into a world where skill with words, which she had neglected for years, was highly valued. Furthermore, she was surrounded by undergraduates who were at least ten years younger than she was and among the sharpest students in the United States. Although she graduated summa cum laude from Stanford and was elected to Phi Beta Kappa, her self-esteem was fragile at this life change.

Nevertheless, after receiving a Master's Degree from the University of California at Riverside, she taught psychology at The City College of San Francisco, where she apparently appeared confident to her students and colleagues. But a personal crisis in 1983 led to her recognizing that she had underlying issues of self-esteem, and to re-evaluating her life and then creating a course called "The Psychology of Shyness and Self-esteem." She also created and led a support group for members of the class, who attended picnics, movies, concerts and parties together.

Now retired from the College and living in her birth town of Minneapolis, she resides in an 1888 Victorian house with a big porch overlooking a lake and a splendid garden. As a confident introvert, she has a small circle of very close friends with whom she shares deep thinking, deep conversations and a lot of fun.

Committed to helping others develop the calmness, clarity, confidence and courage to live a full life, she now provides individual coaching, seminars, and helpful advice in a weekly ezine. She regularly receives rave reviews for her speaking appearances.

For more information about these programs, and to sign up for the weekly ezine, visit CreativeLifeChanges.com.

A nationally acclaimed speaker, Lynette is available for speaking engagements and can be reached through her publisher at CreativeLifeChanges.com.